Come sailing

D1514225

Independent Television Books/Arrow

Come sailing

Peter Copley

Illustrations by
Robin Anderson

Independent Television Books/Arrow

Jointly published by
INDEPENDENT TELEVISION BOOKS LTD
247 Tottenham Court Road, London W1P 0AU

and

ARROW BOOKS LTD
3 Fitzroy Square, London W1

An imprint of the Hutchinson Publishing Group

London Melbourne Sydney Auckland Wellington Johannesburg and agencies throughout the world

First published 1977
© Peter Copley 1977

Cover photographs by
Peter Smith

ISBN 0 09 915510 9

Made and printed in Great Britain
by The Anchor Press Ltd
Tiptree, Essex

Contents

Introduction to sailing

Glinting spray, brightly coloured sails and the sound of wind upon the rigging is a common sight along any open stretch of water. For sailing has now become a major leisure activity and sailing clubs have sprung up wherever there is sufficient water to float a boat. You will find them along the coastline, on tidal estuaries, gravelpits, natural lakes, on rivers and on the Broads. Sailing ranks with golf, tennis and fishing as a major participator sport and a recent survey revealed that more people are afloat each weekend than all those who watch football on a winter weekend.

Most sailing clubs come to life at the weekend, their calendar extending usually from Easter until autumn. In recent years, though, a hardier breed of yachting enthusiasts has emerged. Wearing warm neoprene wet-suits and equipped with maintenance-free glassfibre boats they race the whole year round and so justly earn the title of 'frostbite sailors'.

No matter where you live you will find a sailing club within a few miles of home. A weekend visit will give you a clearer picture of what sailing is all about, for you will be able to see the boats in action and later, when they come ashore, inspect them at close quarters. Dinghy owners are enthusiasts and generally will be pleased to tell you all about the boats they sail.

The best way to get started is to join a sailing club. You will quickly find out if life afloat is really what you want. The club secretary will tell you all about the club, membership costs and the types of boats sailed. But the recent boom in small boat sailing has in many cases over-taxed the facilities available and some clubs have waiting lists for boat owners' membership. It is often possible to join immediately as a crewing member, transferring later to full boat ownership when a boat berth becomes vacant.

Crewing membership gets you afloat in a variety of craft without the expense of actually buying a boat. Crewing under the guidance of an experienced helmsman is invaluable training in the technique of small boat handling. A good skipper will teach his crew how to trim the sails, where to sit and how to cope with weather changes and many of the other problems which arise when sailing a small boat. This knowledge will be of great value when you buy or build your own sailing boat.

Don't expect your local club to possess palatial premises. Most of them have just a clubroom, changing rooms and perhaps a small kitchen serving hot drinks between races. Clubs with superb facilities are often built by the local water authorities alongside new reservoirs but the subscriptions are much higher and they cater for perhaps 1000 or 1500 members. If you have trouble locating a suitable club the Royal Yachting Association (RYA) publishes a full list, county by county, and this is available by post at a small charge (address page 125).

For the beginner sailor who is not attracted by sailing clubs but who prefers solitary cruising along the coastline and into sheltered estuaries, lessons at a qualified sailing school are recommended. Many sailors learn the skill of seamanship by attending one of the RYA recommended sailing schools which are situated around the country. A number of them are fully residential and combine an intensive sailing course with the relaxation of a holiday atmosphere. The RYA will, for a small fee, provide a complete list of these schools.

In addition, night school courses, further education classes and the National Sailing School at Cowes (address page 125) all offer tuition in sailing, navigation, safety and racing. Many local schools include sailing as part of their sports timetable and it forms a part of scouting, adventure training and the Duke of Edinburgh's Award Scheme. Banks, universities and industrial companies often have their own sailing associations and for those who seek the most adventurous experience, there is the Sail Training Association (STA) (address page 125). The STA operate several tall ships such as the *Winston Churchill* and the *Malcolm Miller* and their summer cruises are manned by novice crews whose only qualification is a love of the sea.

Annual exhibitions, such as the National Boat Show at Earl's Court, the London Dinghy Exhibition or the excellent provincial shows at Southampton, Birmingham or Harrogate, offer a further chance of comparing different models and talking to the enthusiasts who both make and sail them. Details of forthcoming exhibitions are usually given in the yachting magazines.

Chapter 1
The theory of sail

Early sailing boats—Roman galleys, Viking long-boats and the later square riggers—all hoisted their sails broadside across the boat, and allowed the wind to drive them directly downwind. Their underwater shape could not prevent these boats from drifting sideways if the wind did not blow directly from behind. This leeway could be so severe that ships' captains might spend many weeks in port awaiting a favourable wind. Indeed it was only the plentiful supply of slave labour chained to the oars which made any progress against the wind possible.

The great breakthrough came when boatbuilders developed the use of fore and aft rigs. The square sails became triangular, the hulls sleeker and deep, heavy keels were hung to sustain the sideways wind forces and minimize the leeway. This improved equipment enabled mariners to use the wind's force to much greater effect, sailing often to within forty-five degrees of the wind's direction. This new-found power allowed them to set sail at almost any time.

Though a boat cannot sail directly into the wind, it can use the wind's power and the boat's shape to squeeze to windwards by setting its sails at an angle which converts the wind's energy into thrust along the boat. The hull design then converts the thrust into forward motion.

Correctly set sails form an airfoil section remarkably similar to that of an aircraft wing. Forward motion causes the air to flow along either side of this airfoil and the resultant difference in pressures generates lift. Most sailing boats have at least two sails—the headsail (jib) and the mainsail. When correctly set upon the mast they form a unified airfoil section but one with an important difference. The 'slot' formed where the jib overlaps the mainsail acts as a *venturi* which speeds up the flow of air and so increases the airfoil's efficiency.

A *venturi* is a shaped funnel through which passing air is both smoothed out and speeded up. It is important to realise that the angle at which the jib is set towards the mainsail controls the size of the *venturi* and thus the performance of the boat. If the angle is too wide then the air is not speeded up enough and the

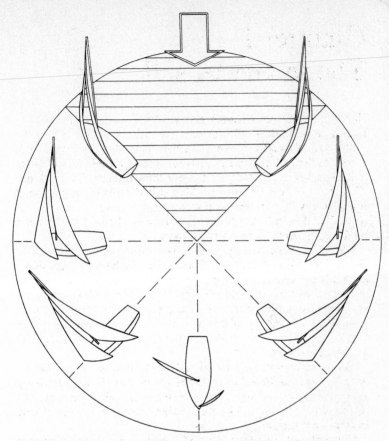

The Points of sailing. Clockwise from 2 o'clock: beating, reaching, broad reaching, running—all on port tack. Then broad reaching, reaching, beating on starboard tack. Wind is blowing from 12 o'clock and hatched zone is a 'no-go' area

mainsail efficiency is reduced; too narrow and it will create turbulent air which backwinds the mainsail and reduces its driving power.

The total force produced by the correctly adjusted airfoil can be resolved into forwards and sideways (or heeling) components. When the sails are tightly trimmed in order to drive to windward the ratio is about five parts of heeling force to only one of forward force. If the sails are eased out from the centreline in order to meet the wind at a broader angle then the heeling force is reduced and the forward force increased. Whether to sail close towards the wind but at a slower speed, or on a longer course but at a higher speed has always been the problem facing helmsmen and navigators.

Tightening in the sails as much as possible enables the boat to sail at approximately forty-five degrees towards the true wind. But as the boat travels forward it also generates a reciprocal wind from dead ahead and this combines with the true wind to form a third force termed the 'apparent wind'. This wind is the real driving force and it moves further and further towards the bows of the boat as the boat's speed increases. The masthead burgee (flag) indicates the direction of the apparent wind and it is in parallel to this that the sails are always trimmed.

Modern sailing boats all employ slim bow sections coupled with broad flat sterns. These lines combined with deep keels or centreboards resist leeway and so enable the boat to squeeze up towards the wind. Sailing close towards the wind is termed beating to windwards (see pages 79-84). A destination upwind is reached by sailing for a time with the wind blowing on to the sails from one side of the boat and then changing direction so that the wind comes from the other side. This zig-zag course is called tacking (see pages 76-77) and forms the basis of elementary boat handling. When the wind blows across the side of the boat roughly at right angles to the line of direction then a reaching course is sailed (see pages 85-86). Reaching is the fastest point of sailing because the sideways thrust has risen to its maximum.

Sailing with the wind from behind is called running free (see pages 89-96) and is generally slower than reaching. This is because in most winds the boat is moving away from the wind and so its total apparent force is reduced. Put simply, if the wind's speed is 6 kilometres per hour and the boat's speed through the water is 2 kilometres per hour then the impact upon the sails is reduced to only 4 kilometres per hour.

These briefly are the theoretical outlines of why a boat sails. But our book is about the practicalities of sailing and the pleasure to be enjoyed afloat.

Chapter 2
The parts of a boat

For clarity it is convenient to subdivide small sailing dinghies into three parts—the *hull,* the *spars,* and the *sails* and *sheets.* The hull is the main body of the boat. It carries the crew, supports the *mast* and contains all the operating controls which adjust the setting of the sails. It may be constructed from wood, heat-formed plastic, glassfibre laminates or even polystyrene foam. Much larger yacht hulls are also made from steel, aluminium or concrete. The hull is long and narrow, its length usually about three times its width. Very powerful racing dinghies may have a width totalling half the overall length, which gives them a fat appearance. The width of a boat is called the *beam.*

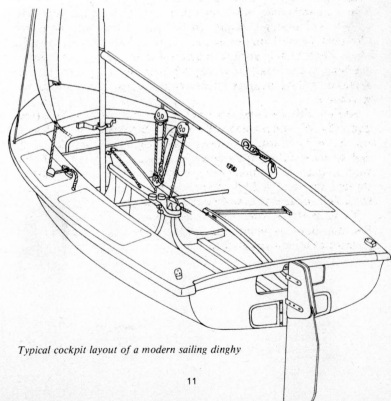

Typical cockpit layout of a modern sailing dinghy

The hull

So that the hull will cut smoothly through the water, the front is tapered to a point—the *bows*. The rear of the hull is much broader and is known as the *stern*. This is often chopped off square and is called the *transom*. The upper surface of the bows may be covered by a *foredeck* which helps prevent spray from entering the cockpit. Beneath this foredeck is dry stowage space and/or integral *buoyancy chambers* which help support the hull if the dinghy capsizes. Narrow *sidedecking* the length of both hull sides serves as both a spray deflector and a seat. Integral air chambers or inflated plastic *buoyancy bags* are situated beneath these side decks. Along the outer edge of the sidedeck is fastened a *rubbing bead* designed to protect the hull in the event of a collision and to prevent damage caused by friction against a mooring or quay.

A *centreboard case,* located in the centre of the cockpit, houses the *centreboard* and a pivot bolt set through this case permits the centreboard to be easily raised and lowered. In some hull designs the centreboard case is replaced by a *daggerboard box*—a much simpler arrangement housing the *daggerboard* which can only be raised and lowered through the vertical plane.

Often a *thwart* runs across the cockpit connecting the inner faces of the hull to the top of the centreboard or daggerboard case. The thwart serves as a seat as well as bracing the hull and centreboard case together into a rigid cruciform unit. *Side seats* screwed onto the upper surface of the thwart often extend down each side of the cockpit. Glassfibre boats may frequently have *buoyancy tanks* bonded onto the inside surface of the hull so that they also act as side seats.

Onto the back of the transom are fastened metal fittings on which the *rudder* is hinged. The lower fitting is called the *pintle* and the upper the *gudgeon*. The rudder consists of a *blade* which is the part submerged beneath the water, a *stock* into which the blade is fastened and a *tiller* which connects with the upper part of the stock. The tiller projects into the cockpit and by moving it from side to side the helmsman can alter the rudder angle and so control the boat's direction. Very often the rudder blade is secured into the stock by means of a single pivot bolt which enables the blade to be lifted when sailing in shallow water. The stock is fitted with matching gudgeon and pintle which are opposite to those fastened on the transom. These all slide

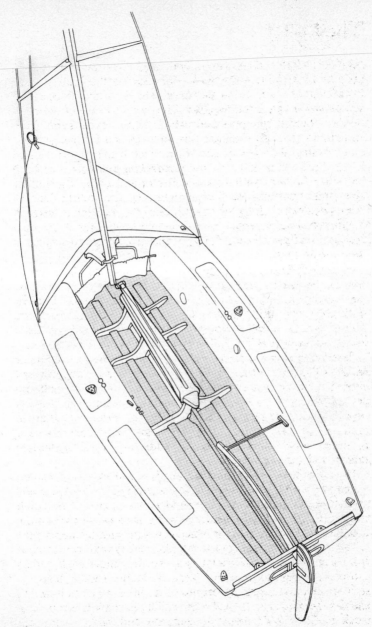

Mast rigging, centreboard layout and crew accommodation plan in medium sized dinghy

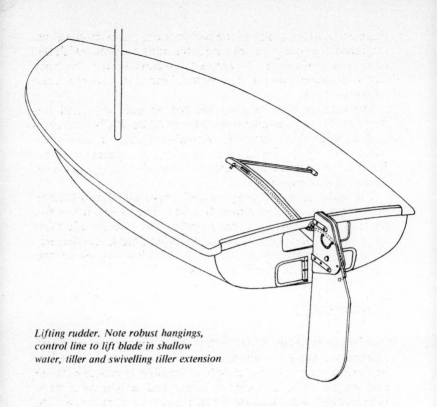

*Lifting rudder. Note robust hangings,
control line to lift blade in shallow
water, tiller and swivelling tiller extension*

together and so enable the rudder assembly to swing from side to side.

Seated within the cockpit and looking forward, the left hand side of the boat is termed *port*, the right hand side *starboard*. Navigation lights are coloured red for port and green for starboard and it is useful to remember that the shorter words (left, port and red) are on one side and the longer words (right, starboard and green) are on the other. The side of the boat upon which the wind is blowing is the *windward* side; downwind is the *leeward* side. Looking towards the bows is facing *forward*; towards the stern is facing *aft*.

Screwed onto the bows is the *stem-head fitting*, a strong anchorage plate onto which the *jib* and *forestay* are secured. Bolted to the hull sides aft of the mast are two further anchorages—these are the *chain plates*. Their job is to anchor the port and starboard *shroud* wires which hold the mast erect.

Fastened onto the centre of the cockpit floor just in front of the centreboard or daggerboard case is the *mast step* into which the base or *heel* of the mast is secured. On some designs the mast step is positioned up on the foredeck, enabling a shorter mast length to be used.

The mast is held aloft by the two shroud wires and the *forestay*. These wires are tensioned with adjustable bottlescrews so that the mast is vertical when viewed from the front and raked slightly aft when viewed from the sides (see pages 113-115). Some boats may use adjustable *shroudplates* or rope *lanyards* instead of bottlescrews.

The sails are adjusted by various ropes all of which have differing names to match their function. The ropes which hoist the sails up the mast are called *halyards*; those which adjust the angle of the sail towards the wind are called *sheets*; and the rest, the kicking strap for example, which in several ways adjust the cloth tension are all called *control lines*.

The spars

The mast is made from either sitka spruce or extruded aluminium. The latest aluminium kind is carefully designed to be flexible and as slim and as light as possible, to reduce windage and weight aloft. Excessive windage and weight aloft both increase heeling momentum which reduces forward thrust. The aft edge of the mast usually has a narrow *luff groove* into which the sail is inserted before being hoisted aloft. The *main halyard* is fastened to the *head* of the *mainsail*, and is led up over a *sheave*, a small pulley, at the *masthead*, down again to another sheave at the *foot* of the mast and finally to a securing *cleat*. By pulling on this halyard, the mainsail is hoisted up the full length of the luff groove until it extends the full height of the mast. The halyard is then secured around the cleat. The *jib* or *foresail* is hoisted in a similar manner using a *jib halyard* which passes over a sheave fastened onto the front face of the mast just below the *hounds*. The hound fitting is a strong collar around the mast about one-quarter of the way down from the masthead. Its purpose is to serve as the upper anchorage point for the two shrouds and the forestay. There is also a very thin halyard running up the mast side for raising and lowering the flag, sometimes called the *burgee*.

The *boom* is also made from materials similar to those used for the mast and usually has a luff groove along its upper surface. The boom is only about one-third the length of the mast and its purpose is to tension the bottom edge of the mainsail. It fastens onto the mast by means of a universal joint called the *gooseneck*.

Sail plan and sheeting arrangements on medium sized dinghy

The sails and sheets

The jib and mainsail, triangular in shape, have three corners named the *head*, *tack* and *clew*. Into each of these corners is set a small metal eye called a *cringle*, through which the various tensioning, hoisting and control ropes are passed. The three sides of the sails are respectively called the *luff*, the *leach* and the *foot*.

Rigging a bermudian-rigged boat

The leading edge (the luff) of the jib is reinforced with a wire luff rope which enables the sail to present a firm straight edge towards the wind. The jib halyard is fastened onto the head cringle either by a knot or a 'D' shaped *shackle*. The tack cringle is secured onto the stem fitting with another shackle and the sail is hoisted until the wire luff rope is tightly stretched. The halyard is then made fast over a cleat near to the mast foot. The *jib sheet* is tied onto the clew cringle midway along its length and one half is led down the portside and the other down the starboard side of the hull. The sheet ends are passed through *fairleads*, which are

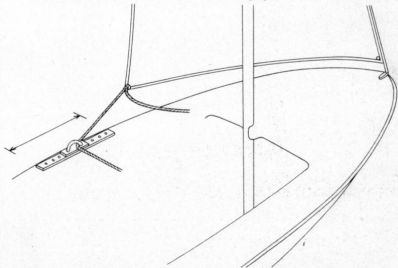

Jib sheet adjustment. It is usual to have the jib fairlead mounted onto a short length of track. This enables fore and aft adjustment to be made in order to match the wind conditions

17

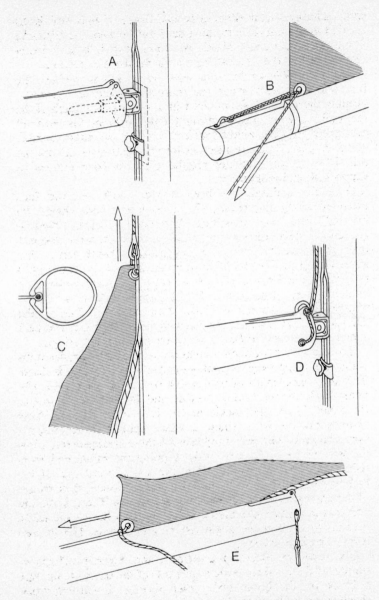

Mainsail controls. a) Gooseneck. b) Outhaul tensioning. c) Mainsail luff groove in mast. d) Tack eye pin securing sail foot to boom. e) Grooved track on upper surface of boom to accommodate bolt rope of sail

small guide eyes set in either deck, and figure-of-eight *stop knots* are tied to prevent them running back out through the fairleads. Some sails have small plastic windows sewn into their lower sections so that the crew can keep a watchful eye to leeward.

The mainsail has a *bolt rope* sewn along both the luff and the foot and this slides inside the mast and boom luff grooves, keeping the sail in close contact with the spars. The leach of the mainsail is cut with a curving *roach* and to prevent this extra sail area from flapping about, battens, made from either flexible wood or glassfibre, are inserted into pockets sewn across the sail. Most sailing dinghies require three or four battens to support the mainsail properly.

Once the mainsail has been hoisted aloft and the foot extended along the boom, the gooseneck spigot should be inserted into the matching boom-end socket. Modern goosenecks slide inside the mast luff groove and can be clamped into any position using an adjustable thumbscrew. The gooseneck should be pulled downwards in the luff groove until the mainsail luff has been correctly tensioned and then fixed by tightening the thumbscrew. The tension is correct when the wrinkles along the sail luff just disappear. The foot of the mainsail should be similarly tensioned along the boom and held in place with a *clew outhaul line* spliced onto the clew cringle.

To ensure that the boom swings across the boat parallel to the water, a *kicking strap*, sometimes called a *boom vang*, is fitted. This is a short length of wire which latches into a keyhole slot beneath the boom, with the other end fastened to a two- or three-part block and tackle at the foot of the mast. Other systems run the wire around a winch spindle which exerts a powerful six-to-one-part purchase. All these arrangements allow the wire to be easily tensioned, stopping the boom end from rising above the horizontal when the sail is eased out. If the kicking strap is omitted or insufficiently tensioned, then the set of the sail will suffer when reaching or running. There is also the risk that in a badly executed gybe the boom will rise and cause the sailcloth to become caught around the shrouds. This mishap is called a Chinese Gybe.

The *mainsheet* controls the setting of the mainsail and is most simply led from a fixed point at one side of the transom, up over a block on the boom end, down through a further block shackled onto the other side of the transom and forward to the helmsman's hand. This arrangement is called a two-part purchase and provides sufficient control for the mainsail in boats up to about four metres in length. Larger craft use extra blocks within the system to gain extra control over the bigger sail. Many boats have their sail controls running from a track screwed across the mid-section of the cockpit up to blocks fastened under the mid-point of the boom. This arrangement, called the centre mainsheet system, gives better sail control than that fastened onto the transom, though it does tend to restrict movement around the cockpits of smaller dinghies.

Rigging gunter-rigged boats

There are many other simpler dinghies whose sail functions are exactly the same but which use much less sophisticated equipment. The most popular is the *gunter rig*, the chief feature of which is a very low main mast. The sail is fastened onto an upper mast called the *gaff* wih *jaws* at the lower ends which embrace the main mast. The main halyard is attached to a point about halfway along the gaff and so hoists both the sail and this upper spar until both are at the top of the main mast. The gunter rig works efficiently only when the gaff is hoisted high enough to reach a vertical position and so closely resembles the bermudian rig already described. The most popular gunter-rigged boat is unquestionably the Mirror dinghy (for details see page 28).

Rigging cat-rigged boats

Even simpler are the cat-rigged, unstayed beach boats. These are nearly all lightweight single-handers designed to be transported on car roof-racks for holiday sailing. The tubular alloy mast is usually in two parts which slip into each other like the segments of a fishing rod. The mainsail does not have a bolt rope but a *sleeve* sewn along its luff instead. This sleeve is slipped over the mast and pulled along its length. The mast is then *stepped* into a strong *mast-pot*, which is bonded into the hull, and is completely unsupported by either shrouds or forestay. The foot is usually loose-footed, the clew simply being tied to the end of the boom and tensioned until the sail takes up a fair curve. Though this is a simple unsophisticated system, there are several high-performance dinghies rigged in this way—the most famous being the single-handed Laser (see page 48 for details).

Chapter 3
What shall I sail?

The earliest sailing dinghies were simply the boat tenders from larger yachts. Later came a limited range of heavy wooden boats suited equally to rowing, fishing or sailing, though these were cumbersome to handle ashore and very difficult to maintain. It is only since the last war, when sailing caught the imagination of so many people, that purpose-built small sail boats have appeared. Today there is a wide choice of boats for cruising, fishing, racing and single-handed sailing, built from low-maintenance glassfibre and equipped with long-lasting synthetic sails.

Such is the variety of choice that the beginner may find it difficult to decide exactly which boat would best suit his purpose. However, there are some decisions which can be made quickly, for most people have fairly clearly defined ideas about size, price and weight. But there are other considerations which may also have a bearing on the decision and these may well eliminate many of the original possibilities.

Overall size is usually a prime consideration, for this determines the number of people able to be carried safely in the boat and, of course, it directly affects the price. Very small boats (between two and three metres) lack cockpit space to accommodate two adults comfortably and the hull will not have adequate buoyancy to support weights in excess of 125 kilos. The small sail will also lack sufficient driving power to push a large weight through the water. So, though a small boat may be cheaply priced, light in weight and easy to store, it would be more suitable for children than for family sailing.

It is worth thinking about the design brief of any boat under consideration. Some family sailing dinghies have been designed as general purpose sailing dinghies, with an eye to racing as well as cruising. If you feel that both these activities may hold an interest for you then something like an Enterprise, a Wayfarer or even the smaller Mirror may be the best buy. Other dinghies have been designed for comfort and stability, without any pretensions to speed and these are obviously more suitable for the family requiring just a cruising and picnicking dinghy for the summer holidays. One of the most popular boats in this range is the Skipper, a 3.6 metre glassfibre dinghy suitable for car-topping, and the larger (just under 4.3 metre) version which is towed on a trailer. Both these boats are deservedly popular with the family sailor because they can easily be rowed, sailed or powered along with an outboard engine.

Sailing dinghies are usually designed either to meet the 'one-design' formula or to comply with the less rigid restrictions of development-class boats. One-design boats are constructed so that each one is identical in every way with all the other boats within the class. In this way the ability of the helmsman assumes greater importance than the complexity of the equipment. One-design boats are not out-dated by latter-day design improvements and so older boats can remain competitive in racing. This type of design always has a very stable second-hand market with an established price structure according to age.

Development-class boats vary greatly, as the class is limited usually to the length of the hull, the area of the sails and the overall weight. There is a tendency for later designs to out-class earlier models completely, with the result that their second-hand value slumps alarmingly. Development-class boats, such as the National Merlin Rocket, International 14 or National Twelve, are strictly for the enthusiast who can afford to experiment, and consequently are not really suitable for the beginner.

Each year many new designs appear on the scene. Some go on to be successful boats like the Mirror and the Laser; others fade away after a few months and are never heard of again. There is much to be said for choosing a well-established boat at first and only making more adventurous choices when greater experience has been gained. A good guide—though not infallible—are the test reports on new boats published by most of the yachting magazines.

Racing boats

Racing boats have to comply with many measurement restrictions which limit the sail area, height of the mast, overall hull dimensions, and the total sailing weight. All these measurements are verified and checked by an official measurer and he then signs a certificate for the boat. Without a valid certificate a boat will not be accepted for racing and most clubs insist that all owners do have valid certificates for their boats.

Never buy a class dinghy without a certificate unless the vendor is prepared to meet the cost of a measurement check as a condition of purchase.

Check that your local club does sail and race the kind of boat you are thinking of buying. If you require more information about a particular dinghy then write to the class association or the builders for further details (see individual boat listings, pages 25-48). Information about cruising boats can be obtained from the Cruising Association (address page 125).

Racing dinghies often sacrifice comfort and low price in the quest for out-and-out performance. They never, however, short-cut on safety for spills are quite likely in these thoroughbred boats. Racing dinghies which gain nationwide acceptance are usually administered by the RYA and are then known as National classes. On rarer occasions an outstanding design might achieve world-wide popularity and then it is administered by the International Yacht Racing Union and becomes known as an International class.

Many sailing dinghies are given a Portsmouth Yardstick Rating number which enables slow and fast boats to race together on a handicap basis. Fast boats have a low number, slower boats a much higher one and, using a set of compensating tables, a race officer can time all the boats over a set course and then use their individual handicap numbers to compute a corrected time. The scheme is administered by the RYA and their annual booklet No. YR2 lists the handicap ratings for most dinghies.

Buying a boat

Because it is so very difficult for a beginner—and many experts, too—to judge whether or not a boat is soundly constructed, there is now an official standard laid down by the Shipbuilders and Boat Builders National Federation (SBBNF) (address page 125). These construction standards ensure that only the highest quality workmanship and materials go into boats in order to meet the requirements. Prospective purchasers should always ensure that their boat has been built in this way and does bear the SBBNF seal of approval.

Annual upkeep is worth considering. Wooden boats have to be painted and varnished regularly if their value is to be maintained. Glassfibre gets by with just an occasional polish, although careless handling can result in glassfibre becoming deeply scratched and some maintenance work is then required.

Early sails used to be made of cotton and quickly lost their shape. They also suffered the ravages of mildew unless they were carefully dried and stored after every sail. Though the odd suit might still turn up with a second-hand boat, cotton sails are not often in use now and their place has been taken by Terylene. This modern synthetic permits more powerful sails to be cut, sails which rarely lose their shape and which can be stored without fear of mildew.

Buying second-hand

Sailing dinghies built from either mahogany planking or marine ply have been available since the war and so there are thousands of second-hand boats available. However, many have been badly maintained and may be a mass of rotting timber (see page 51 for hints on how to judge a second-hand wooden boat). Wooden boats all absorb water and so tend to gain weight over the years. The more modern glassfibre boats tend to retain their original weight but because these boats are so new there are not many second-hand glassfibre boats being offered for sale.

Beginners' boats

Among the small, simple sailing boats suitable for beginners are very small dinghies like the Optimist and, slightly larger, the Gull, the Mirror and the Otter. The selection of beginners' boats which follows is just a cross-section of the better-known craft currently available. There are, of course, many other excellent boats from which to choose.

SHIT

Optimist
International one design
PYR 176

Length overall	2.30 m	(7 ft 7 in)
Beam	1.13 m	(3 ft 8½ in)
Draft	0.08 m	(3 in)
Draft c/b down	0.71 m	(2 ft 4 in)
Mast length	2.35 m	(7 ft 8½ in)
Sail area	3.25 m²	(35 sq ft)
Weight	35kg	(77 lbs)
Construction	wood, glassfibre	
Designer	Clark Mills	

Available in kit form or complete.

The Optimist was designed in Florida and spread via Scandinavia to most parts of the world. It can be cheaply and easily built from a kit and is recommended for children up to the age of fifteen.

Class Secretary: Miss M. Sullivan, 2 Rectory Close, Alverstoke, Gosport, Hants PO12 2HT

Bobbin
One design
No official PYR

Length overall	2.74 m	(9 ft 0 in)
Beam	1.27 m	(4ft 2 in)
Draft	0.08 in	(3 in)
Draft c/b down	0.74 m	(2 ft 5 in)
Mast length	4.57 m	(15 ft 0 in)
Sail area	5.57 m²	(60 sq ft)
Weight	36.28 kg	(80 lbs)
Construction	glassfibre	
Designers	Pearson Bros Ltd	

Not available in kit form.

Sleeved masthead rig with mainsail and jib. May be sailed or rowed or powered with small outboard motor. Suitable for junior sail training or as short-distance transport for adults. Not suitable for racing.

Class Secretary: R.F. Collins, 2 Crown Road, New Malden, Surrey

Mirror ~~SHIT~~
One design
PYR 146

Length overall	3.30 m	(10 ft 10 in)
Beam	1.41 m	(4 ft 7½ in)
Draft	0.15 m	(6 in)
Draft c/b down	0.76 m	(2 ft 6 in)
Mast length	3.20 m	(10 ft 6 in)
Sail area	6.41 m²	(69 sq ft)
Spinnaker	6.08 m²	(65.5 sq ft)
Weight	61.24 kg	(135 lbs)
Construction	marine ply	
Designers	Jack Holt; Barry Bucknell	

Can be supplied complete but most Mirrors are kit-built.

The Mirror was launched in 1963 and 50,000 completed boats had been constructed by mid-1975 and this set a world record. It was intended to be a small family car-top holiday boat but it is now widely used for fishing, cruising, and club racing. Sailed world wide. Can be easily constructed at home from a well designed kit.

Class Secretary: Miss Sally Karslake, Quernmore, Cowbeech, Hailsham, E Sussex

C

Cadet
International one design
PYR 152

Length overall	3.22 m	(10 ft 6¾ in)
Beam	1.27 m	(4 ft 2 in)
Draft	0.23 m	(9 in)
Draft c/b down	0.76 m	(2 ft 6 in)
Mast length	4.50 m	(15 ft 0 in)
Sail area	5.16 m²	(55.5 sq ft)
Spinnaker	4.65 m²	(50.0 sq ft)
Weight	54.43 kg	(120 lbs)
Construction	wood or glassfibre	
Designer	Jack Holt	

Available in kit form, part complete or ready to sail.

The Cadet was originally designed as a training racing boat for young people. Almost 7000 Cadets are now sailed world wide.

Class Secretary: Mrs C. Wood, Tresco, 3 Fern Lea Road, Burnham-on-Crouch, Essex

Gull
One design
PYR 172

Length overall	3.34 m	(11 ft 0 in)
Beam	1.60 m	(5 ft 3 in)
Draft	0.20 m	(8 in)
Draft c/b down	0.91 m	(3 ft 0 in)
Mast length	5.10 m	(17 ft 0 in)
Sail area	6.50 m²	(70 sq ft)
Spinnaker	5.58 m²	(60 sq ft)
Weight	71.58 kg	(160 lbs)
Construction	wood or glassfibre	
Designer	Ian Proctor	

Available in marine ply in kit form or complete in glassfibre.

The Gull is one of the few one-designs which have periodically up-dated their appearance to keep pace with modern trends. This has not affected the one-design characteristics and all the versions still race on equal terms. The latest model is the Mk III with a completely redesigned interior. Sails, spars, rigging and rudder are all interchangeable between the various marks.

Class Secretary: Mr W.P. Stanaway, 9 Wessex Way, Grove, Wantage, Berks OX12 0BS

Otter
One design
PYR 134

Length overall	3.54 m	(11 ft 8 in)
Beam	1.47 m	(4 ft 10 in)
Draft	0.15 m	(6 in)
Draft c/b down	1.06 m	(3 ft 6 in)
Mast length	5.23 m	(17 ft 2 in)
Sail area	6.97 m^2	(75 sq ft)
Spinnaker	5.57 m^2	(60 sq ft)
Weight	74.84 kg	(165 lbs)
Construction	glassfibre	
Designer	O'Brien Kennedy	

Available in part-complete form or ready to sail.

Designed specifically for glassfibre construction, the hull is strongly reinforced with woven rovings which give strength without excessive weight. The recently redesigned interior offers space for two adults and two children when cruising. The Otter is also used for club racing.

Class Secretary: Mr P.F. Warren, Porthole, 19 Slipper Road, Hermitage, Emsworth, Hants.

Cruising and racing

Although there are a few types of small dinghies designed specifically for cruising, most of the boats in this section fill the dual role of cruiser and racer. All are robustly constructed and are much heavier for their size than a comparable boat designed for racing only. The majority have a modestly-sized sail area which allows the boat to be used safely in breezy conditions.

Stability is an important consideration when choosing a cruising dinghy. A stable boat with a high-sided hull makes a safe and dry boat for all the family. Boats which have dry storage compartments are excellent: food, drink and spare clothing can be safely protected from any spray.

If you intend to use an outboard motor with your dinghy then check that the transom is strong enough to cope with the added weight and vibration. The motor is clamped into place with two large thumb screws and these may first have to be packed out with wooden spacers. Spacers are very important on glassfibre boats, otherwise the metal clamps will badly mark the highly-polished surface. Remember to secure the motor to the boat, using either a short chain or a rope lanyard. This will guard against it being lost over the side should it accidentally vibrate off its mountings.

Sailaway
One design
No official PYR

Length overall	3.35 m	(11 ft 1 in)
Beam	1.52 m	(5 ft 0 in)
Draft	0.12 m	(5 in)
Draft c/b down	0.76 m	(2 ft 6 in)
Mast length	4.87 m	(16 ft 0 in)
Sail area	6.68 m²	(72 sq ft)
Weight	62 kg	(136 lbs)
Construction	glassfibre	
Designers	Pearson Bros Ltd	

Not available in kit form.

The Sailaway is designed for rowing, outboarding and sailing and is suitable both for the beginner and for family cruising. It floats very high after a capsize and it is easy to sail under mainsail alone. Suitable for two adults and two children. It is not suitable for racing; hence no PYR has been issued.

Class Secretary: Mr R.F. Collins, 2 Crown Road, New Malden, Surrey

Skipper 12
One design
No official PYR

Length overall	3.66 m	(12 ft 0 in)
Beam	1.45 m	(4 ft 9 in)
Draft	0.15 m	(6 in)
Draft c/b down)	0.76 m	(2 ft 6 in)
Mast length	2.94 m	(12 ft 11 in)
Sail area	6.51 m²	(70.05 sq ft)
Weight	65.77 kg	(145 lbs)
Construction	glassfibre	
Designer	Peter Milne	

Skipper 14
One design
No official PYR

Length overall	4.27 m	(14 ft 0 in)
Beam	1.50 m	(4 ft 11 in)
Draft	0.15 m	(6 in)
Draft c/b down	0.76 m	(2 ft 6 in)
Mast length	3.94 m	(12 ft 11 in)
Sail area	6.51 m	(70.05 sq ft)
Weight	83.92 kg	(185 lbs)
Construction	glassfibre	
Designer	Peter Milne	

The Skipper range of boats marks a new departure in family sailboat design. Peter Milne has designed a boat which is economically priced, roomy inside, maintenance-free, light to move around and simple to rig and sail. Hundreds of Skippers have been sold world-wide and the boat is suitable for up to four occupants in the 12 and five in the 14.

Class Secretary: J. Thornley, 1 Deepdene, Wadhurst, Sussex

G.P. Fourteen
One design
PYR 119

Length overall	4.27 m	(14 ft 0 in)
Beam	1.54 m	(5 ft 0 in)
Draft	0.18 m	(7 in)
Draft c/b down	0.91 m	(3 ft 0 in)
Mast length	7.01 m	(23 ft 0 in)
Sail area	11.35 m²	(122 sq ft)
Spinnaker	7.80 m²	(84 sq ft)
Weight	132.90 kg	(293 lbs)
Construction	wood or glassfibre	
Designer	Jack Holt	

Available in marine ply in kit form or complete in timber or glassfibre.

The G.P. Fourteen was commissioned in 1949 and was the forerunner of most of the currently popular sailing dinghies. The class association keeps a strict watch on technical developments and only sanctions minor alterations to the design if they benefit the class as a whole. Very strict control is maintained on the price of sails, spars and glassfibre hulls. The G.P. Fourteen is suitable for cruising with up to four adults or for club racing with two adults.

Class Secretary: R.H. McCaig, 33 Dougdale Road, Wallasey, Cheshire

Wayfarer
One design
PYR 116

Length overall	4.82 m	(15 ft 10 in)
Beam	1.86 m	(6 ft 1 in)
Draft	0.20 m	(8 in)
Draft c/b down	1.16 m	(3 ft 10 in)
Sail area (cruising)	11.62 m^2	(125 sq ft)
Sail area (racing)	13.10 m^2	(141 sq ft)
Spinnaker	11.62 m^2	(125 sq ft)
Weight	165.57 kg	(365 lbs)
Construction	wood or glassfibre	
Designer	Ian Proctor	

Available in kit form (timber) or complete (timber or glassfibre).

The Wayfarer is an ideal family sailing boat and is used by many sailing schools as their basic trainer. It is heavy and robust and has even been used for long cruises to Iceland and Norway. The Wayfarer will carry up to six adults for short-distance cruising or sail training and two adults for racing.

Class Secretary: Mr F.O. Berry, Alderfen, Neatishead, Norwich NR12 8BP

Drascombe Lugger
One design
No official PYR

Length overall	5.64 m	(18 ft 6 in)
Beam	2.00 m	(6 ft 7 in)
Draft	0.23 m	(10 in)
Draft c/b down	1.22 m	(4 ft 0 in)
Sail area wood	10.68 m²	(115 sq ft)
GRP	11.35 m²	(122 sq ft)
Weight wood	363 kg	(800 lbs)
GRP	386 kg	(850 lbs)
Construction	wood or glassfibre	
Designer	J.L. Watkinson	

The Drascombe Lugger is not available in kit form.

She is a seaworthy family day sailer and can be safely taken out in quite strong winds. The open-plan layout provides a roomy cockpit for at least six people. There is ample locker room and the boat is suitable for sailing, motoring or fishing at anchor. A special outboard motor is available.

Manufacturer: Honnor Marine (Totnes) Ltd, Seymour Wharf, Totnes, Devon

Club racing boats

There are many boats suitable for club racing, ranging from some of the family cruising dinghies already listed to out-and-out racing machines requiring expert crewing. The boats listed below are all suitable for any beginner who has mastered the basic essentials of boat control. Indeed many beginners who wish to start club racing immediately choose one of the these boats even though their initial instability does present some difficulties. It is important to choose one of a class being sailed by your local club. Always check with the club secretary before buying to ensure that your boat will be acceptable.

Tasar
One design
PYR 104

Length overall	4.52 m	(14 ft 10 in)
Beam	1.75 m	(5 ft 9 in)
Draft c/b down	1.53 m	(4 ft 1 in)
Draft	152 mm	(6 in)
Mast length		
(2 pieces)	5.49 m	(18 ft 3 in)
Sail area	11.43 m^2	(123 sq ft)
Construction	glassfibre reinforced with Kevlar 49	
Designers	Frank Bethwaite and Ian Bruce	

Not available in kit form.

The latest two-man racing boat from the same builders as the Laser. Its very light weight is made possible by the careful use of glassfibre lamination work. Can be carried easily on a roof rack. Does not require either a trapeze or a spinnaker and is suitable for husband and wife, young people, adult and child combinations who require high performance without the need for great strength.

Class Secretary: John Heath, Performance Sailcraft Ltd, Swan Close Road, Banbury, Oxon

E

Enterprise
International one design
PYR 118

Length overall	4.04 m	(13 ft 3 in)
Beam	1.62 m	(5 ft 3 in)
Draft	0.18 m	(7 in)
Draft c/b down	0.96 m	(3 ft 2 in)
Mast length	6.20 m	(20 ft 4 in)
Sail area (cruising)	7.43 m^2	(80 sq ft)
Sail area (racing)	10.50 m^2	(113 sq ft)
Weight	90.26 kg	(199 lbs)
Construction	wood or glassfibre	
Designer	Jack Holt	

Available in kit form (timber), part complete (timber or glassfibre), or complete (timber or glassfibre).

The Enterprise is the most popular club racing dinghy in Great Britain. Over 18,000 boats have been built and they are sailed at 450 clubs in the UK plus a further 150 clubs overseas. You can buy a set of smaller sails which makes the Enterprise suitable for family holiday cruising.

Class Secretary: R.J.P. Gumbrell, 18 Chapel Lane, Formby, Liverpool L37 4DU

LARK

Lark
One design
PYR 112

Length overall	4.06 m	(13 ft 4 in)
Beam	1.68 m	(5 ft 6 in)
Draft	0.18 m	(7 in)
Draft c/b down	1.14 m	(3 ft 9 in)
Mast length	6.71 m	(22 ft 0 in)
Sail area	9.75 m^2	(105 sq ft)
Spinnaker	7.43 m^2	(80 sq ft)
Weight	90.71 kg	(200 lbs)
Construction	glassfibre	
Designer	M.P. Jackson	

Available either part complete with glassfibre hull and timber decking, or complete in glassfibre.

Designed for moulding solely in glassfibre, the Lark has achieved considerable popularity with the club racing family man. It is suited to light-weights, husband and wife teams or two youngsters. Service sailing associations, universities and schools have all adopted the Lark as their principal sailing boat.

Class Secretary: Mrs B. Lewis, Vic Lewis Boats Ltd, 10/12 Henshaw Road, Birmingham 10

470

470
International one design
PYR 103

Length overall	4.70 m	(15 ft 5 in)
Beam	1.70 m	(5 ft 6 in)
Draft	0.15 m	(6 in)
Draft c/b down	1.05 m	(3 ft 5½ in)
Mast length	6.86 m	(22 ft 6 in)
Sail area	13.29 m²	(143 sq ft)
Spinnaker	13.01 m²	(140 sq ft)
Weight	118 kg	(260 lbs)
Construction	glassfibre	
Designer	André Cornu	

The 470 was introduced in 1964 and since then the sail numbers have soared world-wide towards the 20,000 mark. The 470 was selected for two-man racing in the 1976 Olympics. She is a very strictly controlled one-design class and, in spite of being an Olympic boat, is quite easy to sail.

Class Secretary: Miss C. Pauley, Haydn House, Terrace Lane, Richmond, Surrey

Single-handers

Perhaps the fastest growing category has been that of the single-handers. Chosen often because they are light and easy to transport on a car roof, the single-handers have mushroomed in the seventies and 'off-the-beach' boats such as the Laser have gained world-wide popularity in a very short time.

Topper
One design
PYR 138

Length overall	3.4 m	(11 ft 2 in)
Beam	1.2 m	(3 ft 10 in)
Draft	0.08 m	(3 in)
Draft c/b down	0.76 m	(2 ft 6 in)
Mast length	5.2 m	(17 ft 0 in)
Sail area	5.21 m^2	(56 sq ft)
Weight	50 kg	(110 lbs)
Construction	polypropelene	
Designer	Ian Proctor	

Not available in kit form.

A popular single-hander in the Middle East, Southern Europe and the USA, the Topper is now gaining popularity in the UK. Although the boat is fast and exciting, its stability and ease of handling make it very suitable for a beginner. The latest boats are machine-moulded and are produced at a rate of one boat every 7 minutes.

Class Secretary: Mr R.L. Hope, Sydney Cottage, Newells Lane, West Ashling, Chichester, Sussex PO18 8DF

Solo
National one design
PYR 122

Length overall	3.77 m	(12 ft 4½ in)
Beam	1.55 m	(5 ft 3 in)
Draft	0.11 m	(4 in)
Draft c/b down	1.04 m	(3 ft 5 in)
Mast length	6.10 m	(20 ft 0 in)
Sail area	8.36 m²	(90 sq ft)
Weight	70 kg	(155 lbs)
Construction	wood or glassfibre	
Designer	Jack Holt	

Available in kit form (timber), part complete (timber or glassfibre), or complete (timber or glassfibre).

A strictly controlled National one-design class which, unusually, has international fleets throughout Northern Europe as well. Suitable for all weights and ages and still a fast-growing class. Very stable but also easy to right after a capsize.

Class Secretary: Mr D.W. Butler, 15 Cherrywood Court, Cambridge Road, Teddington, Middlesex

MS

Minisail
One design
PYR 130

Length overall	3.96 m	(13 ft 0 in)
Beam	1.11 m	(3 ft 8 in)
Draft	0.08 m	(3 in)
Draft c/b down	0.76 m	(2 ft 6 in)
Mast length (2 pieces)	5.94 m	(19 ft 6 in)
Sail area	7.43 m²	(80 sq ft)
Weight	49.90 kg	(110 lbs approx)
Construction	wood and glassfibre	
Designer	Ian Proctor	

Available in kit form (timber) or complete (glassfibre).

The Minisail was one of the first 'off-the-beach' sailing dinghies to achieve real popularity and thousands have been sold world-wide. It is very fast in a blow and yet simple to rig and to sail. It has an optional sliding seat which can be fitted easily to give extra 'sitting out' power. With the sliding seat removed, there is ample room for two people in the cockpit.

Class Secretary: Mrs S. Burgess, 43 St Edmund's Drive, Stanmore, Middlesex

Laser
International one design
PYR 114

Length overall	4.23 m	(13 ft 10½ in)
Beam	1.37 m	(4 ft 6 in)
Draft	0.15 m	(6 in)
Draft c/b down	0.76 m	(2 ft 6 in)
Mast length (2 pieces)	6.46 m	(21 ft 2¼ in)
Sail area	7.06 m²	(76 sq ft)
Weight	68.04 kg	(150 lbs)
Construction	glassfibre	
Designer	Bruce Kirby	

Not available in kit form.

The first production Laser was built in Montreal in 1972. Since then over 40,000 have been sold and mass production factories set up in the UK, Australia, South America and the Republic of Ireland. The Laser is light and responsive with a phenomenal turn of speed. Though favoured by experts, the Laser is easily handled by beginners once they have mastered the rudiments of boat control.

Class Secretary: J. Martin, Swan Close Road, Banbury, Oxon OX16 8AQ

Chapter 4
Your first boat

Novices are well advised to survey every aspect of the sailing scene before buying their own boat. First they should consider where their nearest sailing waters are and the kinds of boat likely to be sailed there. It would be foolish to buy a cruising dinghy if one lived a long distance from the sea and the only local sailing was at a racing club. On the other hand there may be easy access to a safe estuary and in this case a large, stable cruising dinghy would be ideal.

Weekend cruising with just the family aboard and perhaps two full weeks' further use in the summer holidays would suggest a simply rigged glassfibre 'fun-boat', such as the Skipper 12 or the Sailaway. If local club sailing is planned as well as some family cruising then a dual-purpose boat such as the G.P. Fourteen or the Wayfarer would be ideal. If only one or two people wish to use the boat at the same time then a smaller, cheaper and lighter boat like the Otter or the Mirror would be excellent selections.

A careful look at one's basic needs is essential as it is only too easy to make an expensive bad buy. Make every effort to sail in as many different types of boat as possible and try to get a more experienced friend to help you before committing yourself to ownership. Remember that family sailing dinghies lack the speed and manoeuvrability required for racing and that, equally, club racing machines are too unstable and cramped for cruising. There are a few boats which do fulfil both functions but they are the exception rather than the rule. Generally speaking, leisure sailing dinghies are not capable of being tuned up for racing and so it is a waste of time and money to buy bigger sails and more sophisticated equipment for these craft.

These are the basic points which you must bear in mind before finally signing that cheque:

Price The most important consideration. Set a budget before you start and resolutely stay within that figure.

Size Consider how many of you will really want to be out sailing at the same time. Consider, too, the facilities available for storing the boat at home or in the winter.

If you join a sailing club then you should be able to leave your boat inside a lock-up dinghy park throughout the season. It may, however, have to be removed during the winter months and it is as well to check that you do have enough room available to store it at home before you buy. Glassfibre boats can be safely stored outside without much protection but wooden boats do need some cover if their value is to be maintained (see page 120).

Weight To be considered along with size. Will the boat be carried on the car roof-rack or will it be towed on a special road trailer? Bear in mind that trailing will involve you in the expense of having a tow bar, electrical connections and a lighting set as well as the cost of the trailer itself.

The external light socket enables you to plug in the ancillary numberplate and lighting set which must be secured to the back of your boat. Remember that you will be restricted to a lower speed limit when trailing a boat. Roof-rack boats should generally not exceed 68 kilos and include such family boats as the Mirror, the Otter and the Skipper 12. Single-handers such as the Laser and the Minisail also roof-top very well.

If roof-racking is possible, do you have enough strong and willing helpers always available at the end of a strenuous day's sailing to lift the boat back on top of the car?

Construction Bearing in mind the problems associated with winter storage, do you want to spend a proportion of your time in scraping, repairing, painting and varnishing your boat? If the answer is a resounding 'No!' then look for a glassfibre boat. Wood is very attractive to look at but it certainly requires continual care and attention.

Use Family cruising or club racing? Both perhaps? This is a fairly clear-cut decision and may well influence your decisions in the other areas mentioned above.

Once the decisions have been made, you should prepare a short list containing three or four possibles. If the list extends beyond this you must reconsider your objectives again. Boat builders and dealers regularly advertise in the yachting magazines and all will send you brochures, pamphlets and price lists on request. You may be lucky enough to have a knowledgeable boat dealer near to your home and a visit to his showrooms will enable you to discuss and compare your selections with experts.

Obtain as much information as you can. Compare prices, specifications, weights, sail areas and carrying capacity. Find out what optional extras are available — and if any of them are included in the basic price of the boat. Some dealers quote a low price but the boat then needs so-called extras to make it a going concern. Others quote a higher price which is at least the price for the boat in operational trim. These are the questionable areas to which you should give close attention.

Remember that many boats are quoted 'ex sails' and only comparatively few include the sails in the quoted price. This is not sharp practice because many owners prefer to specify their own choice of sailmaker and of course prices vary considerably. It is often a good idea to ask friends sailing boats similar to yours for help in choosing a good sailmaker.

Buying second-hand

A second-hand boat may well be the best way for you to get afloat for the first time. It's certainly cheaper than buying something new. But there are many pitfalls awaiting the inexperienced. An expert sailor can be of inestimable help when buying a second-hand boat, for he can quickly spot the boat's weaknesses. But don't expect too much of him—he is not, after all, a qualified marine surveyor—and don't hold it against him if unforeseen faults show up later.

The classified columns of the yachting magazines list page after page of second-hand bargains. There is certainly no shortage of choice. Read through the lot and then draw up a short list of possibles giving obvious preference to those nearest your home. It's worthwhile considering your local boat dealers too, for many of them also deal in second-hand boats and these may carry a substantial guarantee. Remember that the price quoted usually relates to the age. So a six-year-old boat is obviously going to be offered at a much cheaper price than last year's model. There are always the odd bargains knocking around and you may just manage to pick up a nearly-new boat quite cheaply or a well-maintained veteran for a song but generally you get just about what you pay for.

The next step is to take a look at the possibles selected from the adverts and a telephone call to the vendor is a good idea—if only to ensure that the boat still remains unsold. If the boat is lying in a club dinghy park then a sailing trial should be possible and, hopefully, this should enable you to make a practical assessment of its suitability. It's more likely, though, to be stored at the vendor's home and you will then have to rely on a purely visual inspection. However, by carefully examining each component—the hull, spars, fittings, sails and rudder—it should be possible to arrive at a reasonable evaluation.

If the boat is a class dinghy it should have a registered sail number. These are issued in rotation by the class association and a check with the class secretary will reveal the issue date of that number which will enable you to calculate the boat's age accurately and easily. It should also have a measurement certificate on which at least the sail number and date of construction should be listed although the requirements of the different class dinghies vary quite widely.

It is possible that the boat may exactly suit your needs but does not have a measurement certificate. It might be worthwhile arranging to buy the boat on the condition that a measurement check by an approved measurer will be arranged. If you are interested in club racing then find out if the boat has been raced before. It may have a very good racing record and in this case a small premium might be asked. Beware of paying large premiums for boats with good racing records for much of this success depends on the helmsman rather than the boat.

The hull

A visual check over the lines of the hull will give an indication of the type of life the boat has lived to date. Well-maintained boats have a clean, crisp look about them, but beware the 'quick flash-up' paint job designed to conceal a welter of defects. It is reasonable to expect an older boat to have sustained some damage during its life and well-executed repairs need not be a drawback. It is, however, also reasonable to expect an owner to point these out rather than to conceal them.

Wood rot
Unless the boat was built within the past four or five years then it is unlikely to have a glassfibre hull. Older—and therefore lower-priced—boats use marine plywood for their hull construction and your immediate concern should be wood rot. Many sailing dinghies are built using the hard chine method of construction, in which panels of pre-cut marine plywood are joined together over a building frame to form a hull skin. These

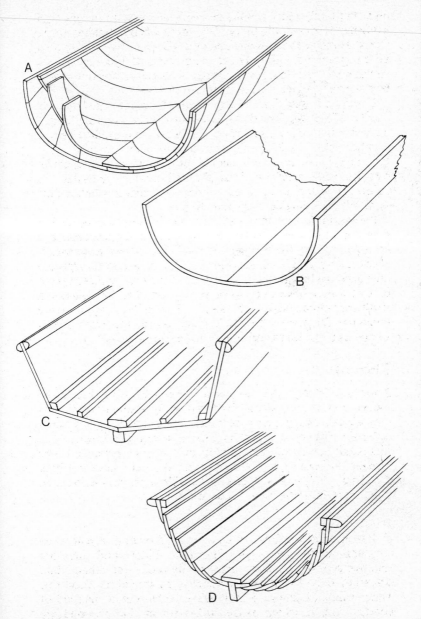

Methods of Construction. a) Cold moulded veneer. b) Glassfibre lamination.
c) Hard chine marine ply. d) Clinker planking

angular joints, called 'chines', run the full length of the hull. Any weakness in the timber is usually found along the chine joints or in the bottom of the cockpit adjacent to the centreboard case.

A few hulls are still made by the clinker process, in which long planks of marine plywood are overlapped onto each other and then glued into place while still on the building frame. Some of the very old boats were made by the 'cold moulding' process, in which thin strips of plywood veneers were glued and stapled over a pre-shaped mould. Further veneer laminations were then added until the skin thickness was built up to the desired strength. This technique has now been largely superseded by glassfibre moulding.

Wood rot in clinker-built boats is caused either by water entering into the hull through a small hole or by bilge water which has been left standing for a long time. It is usually found in the lower parts of the hull and can easily be discerned by the deeply blackened timbers which surround it. Look for it around buoyancy chambers, the centreboard case, stowage lockers or any other dark corner where it can flourish unnoticed. A firm prod with a slim screwdriver will immediately reveal any weakness in these areas. (A similar check along the outside of the hull should be made for peeling or bubbling paintwork.) Fresh paintwork over an area which might contain wood rot could be good cause for suspicion.

The fittings

Built-in buoyancy or inflatable plastic bags must be completely sound. Buoyancy bags can of course be replaced but this is yet another expense and so it is worth checking that the ones on the boat are in good condition. Give the retaining straps a tug to ensure that they are soundly fastened and check after a while that the buoyancy bags do not have a slow leak. All the essential fittings should be present—bow plate, chain plates, mast step, jib leads, halyard cleats and mainsail controls are all basics. Raw screw holes or varicoloured varnish patches may indicate that some fittings might have been recently removed. Check on the reason for this, in the hope that they will be replaced or perhaps a small adjustment to the price made. In any event these missing items might well become a worthwhile bargaining point when haggling over the final price.

The mast

Wooden masts need the closest inspection. A damaged hull can be repaired without too much trouble but a fractured mast will almost certainly have to be replaced. This can be an expensive item and may result in your boat being off the water for weeks if a replacement cannot be readily obtained. The mast should be straight—sighting down from both ends will reveal any twists. The wood may be age-blackened in parts but this doesn't matter if the underlying timber is sound. Cracks running along the grain or in short zig-zags across the grain have been caused by the mast being severely overloaded in high winds. These are compression cracks and unless the boat is being offered very, very cheaply then don't buy—a new mast is required.

Metal masts are not subject to compression cracks but do watch out for deep kinks in the area where the mast tube comes into contact with the foredeck. Shallow indentations are probably acceptable but anything deeper will have weakened the mast. If extra fittings have been installed check for corrosion around the screw holes. Unless the screws have been correctly insulated using zinc-chromate paste (a yellowish-green colour) the subsequent electrolytic action between the fitting and the alloy mast causes corrosion.

The rigging

Check all the standing rigging—shrouds, forestay, etc. Broken strands or kinks in the wire greatly reduce its strength. Replacement costs are not terribly high but, once again, they do open up an area for negotiation. The halyards need similar scrutiny, particularly the jib halyard which undergoes severe loading strain. The wear points to watch for are those where the wire is stretched tight across the sheaves and just behind the splices.

The sails

Second-hand sails will obviously show some signs of wear but generally they should be good for a couple of seasons. The stitching ought to be sound, the batten pockets firmly attached to the sail and in general free from stains or tears. Ignore small repair patches unless you are paying a lot of money for a nearly-new boat. Make sure that the wire rope inside the jib luff is unbroken and that the bolt rope is firmly attached to both the luff and the foot of the mainsail, because a new wire will cost several pounds. Make sure that the plastic window set close to the foot of either the jib or the mainsail is not broken or cracked because this, too, is expensive to replace. A full set of battens of the correct size should be with the sails though these can be easily replaced should one or more be missing. It is a good idea to carry a few spare battens anyway.

The rudder

The rudder blade may well be showing signs of wear, particularly along the leading edge and on the tip, but some work with a plane and file will doubtless soon cure this. Make sure, however, that measurement rules don't prevent this kind of reshaping. Wobble the rudder blade from side to side to see whether there is excess wear in the pivot bolt and check that the tiller fits snugly into the rudder stock. It's a simple job to rectify either of these shortcomings but it's worth noting that a boat-proud owner would not have let them deteriorate in the first place.

Extras

There should be at least a boat cover and possibly a launching trolley and a road trailer as well. However, the existing owner may well be retaining these for use with his new boat so it may be worth asking if they are available to be bought as extras. Covers are usually made from canvas or nylon-reinforced pvc and their state will depend much upon their age. Older covers often have rotted areas in the canvas where the rainwater has collected or rips along the edge where the wind has flogged them against the hull. If the cover is in good condition then regard it as a bonus.

Road trailers may have worn wheel bearings (the wheel can be wobbled from side to side) though replacement bearings can usually be obtained at some cost. The trailer may be rusty and seized up through neglect. The tyres may be smooth. This is illegal, for trailer tyres are subject to exactly the same law as motor car tyres. Such tyres will have to be replaced. Make sure, too, that the trailer is suitable for the size of the boat: too small and the suspension will be dangerously overloaded; too large and it will not support the boat properly and will provide a decidedly hitch-heavy load.

Chapter 5
Building from a kit

There must be countless thousands of part-finished dinghies lying in garages and garden huts—abandoned because their builders simply gave up all hope of seeing the job through to completion. Far better perhaps to sail different boats for a season or so and then build when you have a better idea of what you are trying to accomplish and indeed what the correct results should be! So decide to build your first boat from a kit by all means—but do decide what can be realistically attempted. A successful job will save over one-third of the completed boat price but failure along the way will leave you owning just a heap of very expensive firewood.

Check first on the building space available. You must have a covered building at least two-thirds of a metre longer than the length of the proposed boat with a minimum of the same extra distance on either side. Even the simplest kit will take several weeks to complete so you must have uninterrupted use of that space for a guaranteed length of time. Good artificial light is essential—most boat building is undertaken during the winter evenings, and the space should be clean and relatively free from draughts. Some form of heating is required to ensure that both the glues and the paints dry properly; a minimum temperature of 16°C is recommended.

Select a kit which is within your technical competence—even if it means paying a little extra for some of the harder jobs to be completed by the supplier. Many kits are supplied in varying stages, each additional stage requiring rather less work to achieve the finished result. Suppliers of kits define the extent of each stage in their price lists and they may vary slightly from one firm to the next. Generally, stage I provides all the woodwork with the formers, deck beams and other complex shapes already machined to pattern. Stage II goes further by providing the hull already built, with perhaps the centreboard case installed. Stage III has the deck and side beams installed, leaving just the seating and deck panelling to complete. Stage IV is a finished boat requiring just sanding, painting and varnishing. Glassfibre hulled kits are always supplied at the equivalent to stage IV, with just the fittings left to be screwed down and the spars to be rigged. Obviously there is not much of a saving made when the kit is purchased in these more advanced forms.

Stitch and glue kits

One of the simplest boat kits is the Mirror dinghy of which more than 50,000 examples have already been made. Designed and developed by Barry Bucknell and Jack Holt, the Mirror introduced a simplified form of construction which made it easy for the man with only the simplest set of tools to assemble his own boat. Only the most basic skills are required because all the more usual specialist boat-building techniques have been eliminated from this kit.

The Mirror kit is supplied with pre-cut wooden hull panels, each forming a numbered part in the plans. The bottom panels are laid face to face and a series of closely spaced holes drilled by the constructor along their joining edge. Short lengths of copper wire are twisted through these holes, 'sewing' the panels together. The upper panels are joined onto each side in a similar manner and the two halves opened out like a book. The bow and stern transoms are laced into position and then the buoyancy tanks are inserted which force the hull panels out into their correct shape. All the joints are then sealed with a lamination of glassfibre tape and resin. When this has cured to a hard finish, the protruding twists of copper wire are snipped off and the seam sanded smooth. Not surprisingly, this building technique has been extended to other boats and is aptly called stitch and glue.

All that now remains is to glue the deck panels into place and assemble the rudder, daggerboard and spars before finally sanding everything down for painting and varnishing. The overall building time varies according to skill but a fair average would be about one hundred and twenty hours. Owners who have built more than one Mirror kit can easily reduce this to about seventy hours. The advantage with the stitch and glue system is that it is possible to move the part-complete boat into any convenient corner during its construction, so the long-term need for extensive building space is not so acute.

A recent development has been to provide kits with a series of pre-shaped spacers on which are cut protruding tabs. These tabs are inserted through matching slots machined into the hull panels and enable the kit to be quickly assembled, rather like a child's cardboard cut-out model. This technique allows a visible boat shape to be achieved during the first session, which ensures that the builder's interest is maintained, and overcomes the main reason that so many conventional kits are abandoned: that after many hours of work on essential sub-components, there is still no sign of anything which even resembles a boat!

'Self-jigging' kits

More elaborate are boat kits which rely on self-jigging components to determine the final hull shape. The Fireball is a good example of this building method. The centreboard case and a series of wooden 'girders' are joined together on the workbench to form a backbone for the hull. Along marked positions are hung the transom, buoyancy bulkheads, and other spacers which 'self-jig' the hull shape. Once in position they are checked and double-checked to ensure that they are fixed at the correct angle and distance from each other before being finally glued and screwed into place. The bottom, side and deck panels are then fixed into place, checked all the time to ensure that the shape complies with the building plans. Small tolerances are allowed in these measurements (usually plus or minus five millimetres) but even so a high degree of accuracy is required and a knowledge of woodworking techniques is essential. The total building time would be about one hundred and fifty hours.

Hard-chine kits

Most difficult of all are the hard-chine kits like the Enterprise or G.P. Fourteen. These hulls are assembled upside down onto building frames which can usually be rented from the kit suppliers. It is essential that these frames should be accurately fixed onto a perfectly level floor before any building begins. Once in position they must remain untouched until the hull has been completed—perhaps two hundred hours or more.

Tools needed

A beginner should certainly not attempt one of these kits unless he has a first class set of tools, an excellent knowledge of woodworking techniques and unlimited access to the type of building space described earlier in this chapter. It would be much safer to choose a stage II or stage III kit even though the initial expense will be higher.

Whichever type of kit is chosen, the final result will depend very much on the care taken at every stage. As we have already noted, small sailing dinghies are constructed to quite small tolerances and these just cannot be achieved if early work is wrongly joined together. The motto of the boat building trade has always been 'Measure twice and cut once'.

Simple boats do not require an extensive tool-box and many home builders assemble Mirror dinghies using only a screwdriver, a saw and a hammer. But it does make life easier if the correct tools are readily to hand and the following list should cope with any of the boat kits already mentioned:

panel saw	carpenter's square	smoothing plane
tenon saw	bradawl	spokeshave
coping saw	centre punch	hand drill
ball pein hammer	pliers	mallet
small screwdriver	spirit level	steel rule
large screwdriver	assorted chisels	assorted G clamps

A power drill is almost indispensable, preferably with as many attachments as possible. A high-speed orbital sander can ease the hard work of rubbing down which is needed to achieve that mirror-like finish to paintwork.

Finishing glassfibre kits means little more than just screwing down the fittings using self-tapping screws and small machine bolts. A good power drill and a selection of high-speed drills is essential and, of course, a screwdriver, file and hacksaw.

Chapter 6
What to wear

Choosing suitable clothing is just as important as choosing the right boat. Remember that water is a hostile medium, so never take chances. Warm waterproof clothing, safe sensible footwear and well-fitting life-jackets must be standard equipment on every boat. It is important to have some sort of buoyancy aid for everyone in the boat—imperative for weak swimmers and children.

Many people regard the words 'life-jacket' and 'buoyancy aid' as totally interchangeable but this is not correct. There is a world of difference between the two and you should be quite clear about these differences before making your purchase.

Life-jackets

Life-jackets comply with the highest standards of safety and are designed to float the wearer high out of the water in a face-upwards position. They are constructed out of light-weight foam sealed inside a heavy-duty nylon casing and have a back-up inflation lung which can quickly increase the buoyancy. This lung is inflated by either a miniature CO_2 bottle or simple air inflation. The garment is held onto the wearer's body with heavy-duty terylene straps. It is equipped with a whistle which can be blown in an emergency.

Life-jackets are most suitable for offshore sailing and you should keep a spare jacket available so that any guest sailing with you can be properly equipped. Many school sailing associations insist that their pupils wear life-jackets no matter how skilled they are. It is sensible advice that no one should go afloat who cannot swim. Weak swimmers who go sailing should always wear a top quality life-jacket. Failure to do so places not only their own safety at risk but also endangers the rescue crews who may later have to save them.

Buoyancy aids

Small boat sailors often prefer slimmer-fitting buoyancy aids, which are more comfortable to wear and permit quicker movement within the boat. Indeed, most clubs insist that bouyancy aids be worn at all times. These aids supplement the body's natural buoyancy and keep the wearer afloat until he can right his boat or until help arrives. Most buoyancy aids are much cheaper than life-jackets, though the more sophisticated models can cost almost as much.

The lower priced garments are made from slabs of buoyant foam encased within heat-sealed plastic envelopes. These in turn are heat-sealed inside a plastic waistcoat which is either zipped or laced up the front. Providing that these garments are not torn or damaged in any way they will be quite suitable for inland or inshore sailing. If the outer casing becomes torn or ruptured then the foam will absorb water and its buoyancy will become much reduced.

Better quality—and much higher priced—buoyancy aids use materials which have a greater safety factor. The most popular use narrow slabs of closed-cell polyethylene foam sewn inside a heavy-duty nylon waistcoat. This type of foam is monocellular in construction and so does not absorb water as an ordinary sponge might. It is therefore possible to damage it severely without destroying its buoyant qualities.

Another popular design has scores of small, plastic, sealed-air sachets sewn within the waistcoat casing. Each of these resembles a small shampoo sachet and exerts a strong, buoyant lift when the wearer is in the water. Probably twenty per cent of these self-contained sachets could burst before buoyancy was seriously impaired.

Sailing gear

Many clothing firms produce waterproof sailing gear and there is a wide and colourful choice available. The range covers heavy-duty offshore oilies and extends to light-weight showerproof anoraks. If you plan on going afloat in all weathers then the heavy-weight garments will be your best choice. They can be obtained in heavy-duty plastic with heat-welded seams or in five-ounce nylon with double-sewn seams. Both types use non-corrosive zips and they usually have overlapping zip flaps to prevent spray seeping through the teeth. There is at least one pocket sealed with a Velcro flap and several have a transparent course card pocket on the thigh.

Undemanding conditions require only light-weight nylon to

keep out the weather and so most inshore dinghy wear is tailored from either two-ounce or four-ounce nylon cloth. These are fairly cheap, much lighter and less susceptible to condensation. They are available in bright colours—blue, red, yellow and orange are the most popular shades—though the Royal Society for the Prevention of Accidents (RoSPA) is anxious to see the maximum use made of Day-glo fluorescent orange. Bright colours are easy to spot in the event of an accident—a good reason for not wearing dark green or dark blue.

There is a variety of styles to choose from. The most popular is the traditional smock with a short front zip and a full-width chest pocket. There is also a similar garment with a full-length front zip and two side pockets which has become popular because it can be worn coat-style rather than having to be dragged on and off over one's head. Either style can be worn with matching trousers. Trousers can also be bought with chest-high bib fronts, which are most useful in rough weather for they ward off the spray which tends to seep up between the anorak bottom and the normal trouser waistband.

A combination popular with children is the pouch pack which ingeniously employs the anorak pocket as a carrying container for the trousers and the anorak itself. The rolled-up pack measures only 150 mm by 100 mm and can be carried on the child's belt. The material is very light-weight and is therefore only showerproof.

Racing dinghy crews have shown a strong preference for heavy-weight nylon overalls—which have an elasticated waist, close-fitting neck and waterproof pockets, which are positioned so that the course card, racing stop-watch and other gear can be conveniently stowed. The close-fitting nature of the garment prevents water from finding its way through at the waist and its smooth outline reduces the possibility of clothes snagging in the rigging. They are cheaper than the combination of anorak and trousers—though not as adaptable. The experts favour them and there is no reason why the beginner should not find them just as useful.

Footwear

Footwear is very important and several firms produce a range of specialist sailing shoes. These have a non-slip tread bonded onto a light-weight canvas upper and are available in a wide range of sizes. Some sailors prefer close-fitting boxing-type boots made from waterproof plastic laced up over a waterproof gusset. Another popular shoe is the sailing boot which is made from warm neoprene rubber bonded inside a non-slip boot. This boot traps a thin layer of moisture—perspiration or sea water—between the wearer's skin and the boot and this moisture quickly heats up to blood temperature. The effect is similar to having a small immersion heater inside your shoe. Finally, for the less fashion conscious—and more cost conscious—there are the old gym shoes worn on bare feet which are more than adequate for summer sailing.

All-year-round sailing gear

There is no doubt that the introduction of diving wet-suits has done much to make sailing into an all-year-round sport. Like the boots described above, they trap a thin layer of moisture between the skin and the suit and this, when warm, is protection against all but the coldest weather. Sailing clubs which promote winter race meetings stipulate that all competitors must wear wet-suits. (This is a prudent rule because in the event of a capsize into cold water, death by exposure can be very quick indeed and the risk just isn't worth taking.) It is of course compulsory that life-jackets be worn as well—neoprene wet-suits are not considered buoyant enough to act as buoyancy aids alone.

The latest wet-suits for sailing wear have been especially designed for the job, whereas the earlier ones were just the same as those used for underwater work. For surface water sports in most conditions the lighter three-millimetre neoprene, bonded on both sides with nylon, is quite adequate. It is certainly more comfortable to wear and allows much easier movement than the heavier versions.

The most popular style is the two-piece suit comprising a long-sleeved jacket and a matching pair of trousers. Equally popular among dinghy sailors is the Long John, which is a one-piece suit without either collar or sleeves. The Long John can be worn in conjunction with a woolly sweater on cold days or a thin, cotton T-shirt in the summer. Both the suit and the Long John are usually worn with either sailing boots or neoprene wet-socks. The other popular style is the Shortie—a jacket with shorts attached. It does have the shortcoming of leaving the legs exposed to the vagaries of the climate and this can prove to be very cold indeed when out at sea.

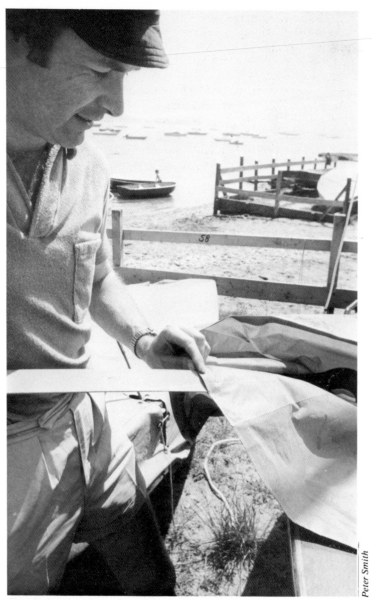

Inserting the sail battens

Feeding the mainsail into the mast luff groove

Peter Smith

Making sure the tiller fits snugly into the rudder stock
Checking that the lifting rudder blade moves smoothly up and down

*Ready to launch. Note rudder blade lifted, bungs in position, sails
lowered. Always launch stern first*

Launching from the beach. Note how crew holds bows of the boat towards the wind. Launching trolley in foreground should be removed above high water mark

Launching from a pontoon. Sails up and ready to leave. Though there are many willing helpers around, it would have been better to have rigged the Solo dinghy on the leeward side of the pontoon

Beating to windwards in moderate breeze. Note the helmsman seated up on the weather side where he can both balance the boat and also obtain a clear view all around. Crew sits in the middle of the cockpit ready to move to either side should wind force change

Running Goose-winged. Helmsman is seated to weather where he can obtain best all round vision. Note that jib stick keeps the jib properly set and that crew holds the main boom out. Weight well forward to lift broad rear hull sections clear of the water

A close fetch to windwards in a strong wind. Note both helmsman and crew are seated well out on the windward side. Lack of spume from rudder blade indicates that the boat is well balanced

Trapezing on a close reach under spinnaker. See how the crew is out at right angles to the boat; the helmsman should move a little more towards the windward side in order to bring the boat level

Spinnaker set on a broad reach. The spinnaker pole set on the windward side is tilted a little too high; both clews of the spinnaker should be level

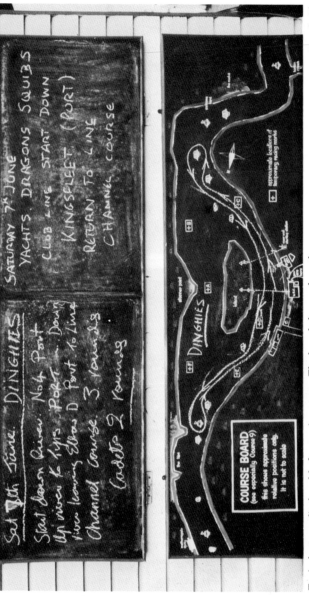

Typical course displayed before racing starts. The board shows where the rounding buoys are, the order in which they are to be rounded and the number of laps to be sailed

Peter Smith

Peter Smith

*Running down to the leeward mark. F2223 is being blanketed by F3415
who will soon draw level. Unfortunately the roles will be then reversed and
F3415 will fall into his pursuer's wind shadow. It is best to overtake just
before passing round the leeward mark*

K11376 still has luffing rights over K15410 and could suddenly swerve up to windward striking a glancing blow. Luffing rights cease when the helmsman of K15410 seated in his normal position draws level with the mast of K11376

*Overlap at the mark—a tricky situation. 1025 must move over to allow
1890 to correctly round the mark. BUT 1890 is only entitled to this if he
gained an overlap on 1025 two clear boat lengths before the mark was
reached*

Peter Copley

Due to wind shadowing 11720 is overtaking 3844 who in turn is overtaking 2149. In fact 11720 is out in the strong adverse river current and will soon fall back allowing 2149, in the slack water, to creep ahead again

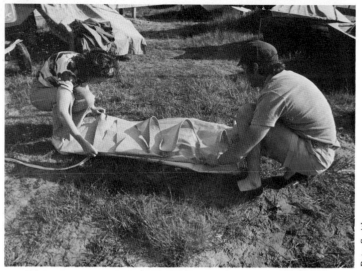

Fold the mainsail parallel to the foot taking care to vary the folds on each outing, or permanent creases tend to develop. Finally, fold the sail a few times crossways so that it will slip easily inside the sailbag

Coil the jib around its luff wire making sure that the plastic window is folded on the outside of this bundle. This precaution is very necessary in winter because the plastic hardens and may crack if the folds are too tight

Many sailors now make their own wet-suits and several excellent kits are available. The better ones have clearly marked out patterns and come complete with glue, zips, sealing tape and full cutting instructions. Beware of some of the cheaper kits, for they are often no more than a roll of neoprene without glue or instructions. Always inspect the contents of any kit before buying.

Never be misled by warm conditions on shore. It is always much colder out at sea and some warm clothing should be taken aboard inside a waterproof holdall or a well-sealed plastic bag. A few woollen sweaters, a spare pair of jeans and a light-weight anorak will clothe anyone needing extra protection or dry clothing in the case of an accident.

Chapter 7
Launching and recovery

Launching a new boat is a memorable occasion whether it be a supertanker or a home-built dinghy. Some owners stage elaborate ceremonies complete with champagne; others rush their latest dinghy into the water just before the starting gun and probably win the first race. Whichever technique you adopt, do remember to put the drain bungs in first!

Before launching your dinghy into the water for the first time make sure that all the rigging has been securely fastened down. It is a good idea to make up a short check list which can be run through during the early days until natural familiarity with your boat has been attained.

Make sure the mast is properly seated in the step and that the shrouds and forestay are firmly anchored into place. Check that the sails are firmly shackled to the halyards ready for hoisting and that the mainsail is already secured onto the boom. A bailing bucket, a small plastic scoop and perhaps a sponge should always be within the cockpit; and never go to sea without an anchor and at least thirty metres of suitable line.

Though a small dinghy can be carried into the water with the aid of a few helpers it is much simpler to use a launching trolley. These are usually made from tubular steel which is either painted or, better still, hot-dipped galvanised to resist the ravages of salt water. A wide variety of wheels is available, ranging from small, solid, rubber ones suitable only for smooth concrete launching ramps, to large-diameter plastic rollers designed for soft sand. The best all-round performance is offered by pneumatic 406mm × 102mm tyres which cope with most surfaces. These wheels are fitted onto plain axle bearings which must be kept regularly greased.

The axle is fitted with either two shaped chocks or, preferably, a shaped plastic cradle which snugly supports the hull. A carrying handle extends around the bows which makes it easy to move the boat without stooping.

The jib is usually hoisted before launching but it is safer to leave the mainsail lowered unless the wind is very light. It should, however, be already tensioned along the boom with the battens inside their pockets so that it can be hoisted rapidly once the boat is afloat. A short length of rope of about two metres should be tied at one end to the bow plate and lashed around the trolley handle to keep the hull in place during the short journey to the water. This rope will also serve as a painter for tying up alongside a jetty or onto a mooring buoy.

Always launch the dinghy stern first for this will enable it to float clear of the trolley in quite shallow water. If the boat is launched bow first you will have to precede the boat into the water and may be waist deep before it floats clear off the trolley. Have your crew take the trolley out of the water and return it to a safe place above the high-water mark. This elementary precaution is frequently overlooked and one can often see trailers and trollies lying beneath the water around a slipway, left by unthinking owners as they rush out to the sea. You, in the meantime, should hold the boat by the painter so that it faces into the wind.

When the trolley is safely stowed instruct the crew to hold the boat at the bows by the forestay, letting it swing freely downwind—whilst you hoist the mainsail. Novice crews should clearly understand that their job is to act as a fixed pivot point and not to resist any wind or current forces on the hull. Once the mainsail has been hoisted, cleat the halyard, let the sheet run out until the sail is flapping, attach the gooseneck to the boom and tension the kicking strap. Make sure that the battens are correctly inserted, that the line tensioning the sail along the boom is taut and securely fastened, and that the tack eyepin is firmly in place.

Taking a quick look, check the depth of the water. If it is deep enough, insert the rudder, ensuring that it is firmly seated on its hangings and that it is free to swing from side to side. A quick tug on the tiller will confirm that it is secure within the stock and a similar tug on the rudder uphaul/downhaul lines will indicate that the rudder can be easily raised and lowered. Check that the mainsheet is not twisted or fouled; check that the jibsheet is not trapped in a jamming cleat. A final look along the cockpit floor confirms that it is free from a clutter of paddles, bailing buckets or spare clothing.

When all this is done, take a final look at the sails. Correctly hoisted? Good. Masthead burgee? Flying freely. No other sailing boats in the near vicinity? All clear. It's time to cast off and head for the open water. One *warning:* if you are launching from a busy holiday beach keep a sharp eye open for small children playing and swimming along the water's edge. Small bobbing heads are easy to overlook—particularly on a bright sunny day.

The bows are eased away from the wind and as it starts to blow into the sails the crew climbs into the cockpit and positions himself where he easily balances the boat. The helmsman, still in the water at the rear of the boat, gives it a hard shove and, as it gathers speed, climbs into the cockpit as well. He immediately takes control of the tiller with the hand nearest the transom and hauls in on the mainsheet with his other hand.

With an offshore wind the boat will move swiftly out into deeper water where the centreboard can be lowered in its case to its full depth, and also the rudder, if it has not already been lowered.

Onshore winds are more difficult for it will be necessary to tack from side to side until deeper water is reached. This will obviously take a longer time and, to make matters worse, the partially raised centreboard and rudder will cause considerable leeway (sideslip) to be made. It is important, therefore, for the crew to ease the centreboard down continually to take advantage of every bit of deepening water.

Returning to shore

The reverse procedure takes place when returning to shore. An onshore wind will bring you back in a hurry and it is sensible to head into the wind and lower the mainsail when you are still a safe distance offshore. If you need to slow down, allow the jib to flap. It is then a simple matter to sail into shallow water under the power of the jib alone. Surprisingly, a sandy beach does not ensure a soft landing. Coming into a beach under full sail produces an impact which feels more as if you had run into a brick wall.

An offshore wind permits you to tack from side to side under full sail until the shelving beach can be felt touching the centreboard tip. The centreboard can then be hoisted gradually. When the water becomes shallow enough, turn head to wind, let the sails flap and allow the crew to leap overboard. He can then hold the head of the boat into the wind. Make sure the rudder blade has been lifted as the water becomes more shallow.

Landing against a jetty is rather more difficult because one is aiming for a specific point. An offshore wind allows you to tack slowly towards the jetty until the sails are slacked off and the crew leaps nimbly ashore. It is important that he does so with the mooring line in his hand or the boat might easily float away again. Downwind the safest course is to come into the wind, lower the mainsail and then come alongside under jib power alone. Even this sail can generate a lot of power and may have to be slackened off for the last metre or so.

Once ashore or moored, the sails should be lowered as quickly as possible and secured inside the cockpit so that they cannot be blown into the water by a puff of wind. Always pull the sails down along the luff ropes; tugging at the leach can quickly ruin the sail. Unship the rudder, placing it with the tiller inside the cockpit, and ensure that the centreboard is fully retracted inside its case. If your boat is fitted with self-bailers then make sure that these are now fully closed. Run the boat into slightly deeper water so that the launching trolley can engage under the bilges, tie the mooring line around the trolley handle and then pull the boat up onto dry land. If there is a strong cross-current it may be necessary for the crew to wade into deeper water in order to hold the boat firmly in place on the trolley.

Wash the whole boat down with fresh water and make sure that the sails, spars and rigging receive their fair share. Coil up the halyards, making sure that loose ends are not left flogging against the mast and coil the sheets or even remove them from the boat. Dry the sails before stowing them away—flying them loosely from the masthead is a good method. Coil the jib around its luff wire making sure that the plastic window is folded on the outside of this bundle. This precaution is very necessary in winter because the plastic hardens and may crack if the folds are too tight.

Fold the mainsail parallel to the foot taking care to vary the folds on each outing, or permanent creases tend to develop. Finally, fold the sail a few times crossways so that it will slip easily inside the sailbag. A large open-topped sail valise is even better because it allows you to stow away the sail without crushing it through a narrow neck. Always take special care to stow the battens flat, otherwise they develop permanent bends.

Cover the boat with a plastic or canvas boat cover—most builders supply a specially tailored model which is called a boom-up cover because it drapes across the boom and so sheds any rainwater. A deep-skirt protects the side of the hull and under-tie ropes keep it firmly in position. Raise the bows with a wooden prop so that the transom rests against the ground, preferably cushioned by an old motor tyre. Open up the rear drain bungs and any buoyancy tank bungs so that bilge water can swiftly drain away. Finally, lash the boat down to stakes driven into the ground on either side of the hull.

Chapter 8
The first sail

The three fundamentals of boat control are sail handling, steering and balance. Though each can be discussed separately they are for practical purposes completely interrelated. Sail handling acts both as the accelerator and, to a lesser degree, the brake. Steering controls the direction of the boat and also ensures that the sails remain correctly angled to the wind. Balance is crucial, for the continual movement of crew weight within the cockpit offsets the varying wind pressure against the sails.

The helmsman should always place himself on the windward side of the cockpit, counterbalancing the thrust of the wind on the sails.

Let us assume that our boat is sailing on port tack. That means that the wind is blowing from over the left-hand side (port) of the hull and consequently the sails are swung out towards the right-hand (starboard) side. The crew tightens his starboard jib sheet so that the angle of the foresail narrows towards the centreline of the boat. At first the sailcloth will be shaking loosely, particularly along the luff of the jib. As the jib sheet is pulled tighter this shaking will diminish until the cloth finally lies quiet. This is called 'putting the jib to sleep' and the crew's main task is to set and reset the jib constantly in this manner.

The helmsman simultaneously sheets in the mainsail until the luff lies quiet on his sail as well. Because his mainsheet runs through several blocks, several handfuls of rope may have to be withdrawn before the sail adjustment is correct. A good rule of thumb is to adjust the angle of the boom towards the boat's centreline until it matches the angle of the burgee flying at the masthead.

Remember that the tiller is always controlled by the hand nearest it. At first it is very difficult to steer the boat with one hand and adjust the sail sheeting angle with the other. The effect is that the boat will weave about from side to side—the reaction to pulling in large handfuls of rope with one hand and overcompensating the tiller direction with the other. Constant practice will, of course, cure this fault but it helps to lead the

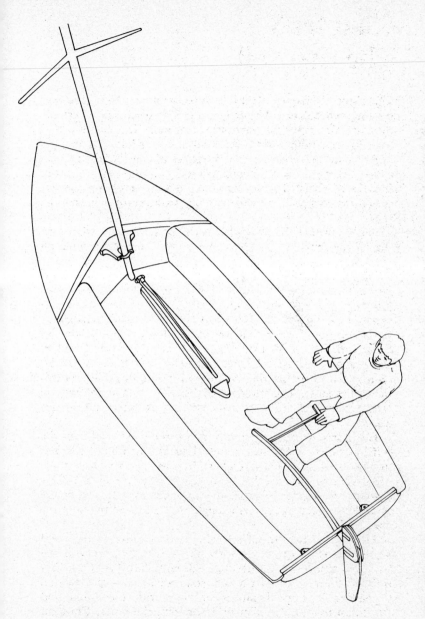

Normal position for helmsman in moderate conditions. Lighter airs would see him seated further forward; heavier winds would dictate a position further aft

mainsheet first through the fingers controlling the tiller (the right hand on this tack) and thence across the body to the left hand. Trimming the mainsail is now more easily accomplished by pulling in a length of rope with the left hand and stopping it with the right. The left hand then takes in another length of slack which is again stopped by the right hand. The haul-and-stop method enables long lengths of sheet to be taken in quickly without affecting the steering.

The sails should never be pulled in to the required setting and then left, for the wind strength and direction will be continually changing. The setting must be constantly checked by easing out the sheets a fraction until the luff starts to shiver and then tightened in until all is quiet. This constant trimming ensures that the sail's angle towards the wind is always at its optimum. Guard against the tendency to pull in the sheets more than necessary.

The rudder angle controls and alters the boat's direction. Pulling the tiller across the boat towards the helmsman turns the

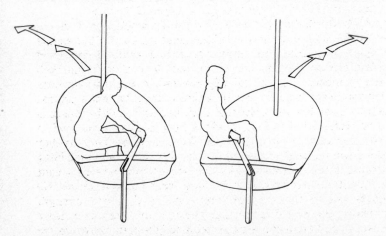

Tiller control. Pushing tiller away heads boat into wind. Pulling tiller across turns boat away from the wind

bows away from the wind. Pushing it across the boat away from the helmsman brings the bows towards the wind. It is important to realize that steering with a tiller reverses all land-based steering systems—pushing the tiller to the left turns the boat to the right. This reverse action feels very strange to everyone taking the tiller for the first time and it is worthwhile to practise on an open stretch of water.

The setting of the tiller and the angle of the sails work in close relation with each other. Move the tiller gently towards you until the wind can be felt blowing across the port side of the hull. Keep adjusting the tiller setting until the wind blows squarely onto the sails from a position at right angles to the centre line. This wind direction is called abeam. The mainsail and jib sheets can be adjusted—in or out—until the sail's luffs lie just asleep. The boat is now perfectly set up for broad reaching—the easiest course to sail.

If the wind is blowing across the side of the boat from abeam and the sails are still flapping loosely, then there are two remedies. Either trim the sails closer, as already described, until they lie quiet or, alternatively, pull the tiller further across the cockpit towards you, which will move the boat away from the wind and so fill the sails. Flapping sails—the technical term is luffing—are an indication that the steering direction and sail settings are mismatched in relation to the wind direction.

Small dinghies do not employ heavy stabilizing keels to maintain balance but rely upon the rapid transfer of live weight around the cockpit to adjust the sailing angle. Extra wind pressure upon the sails causes the boat to heel over and both crew members must immediately move their weight across onto the windward side to counterbalance this. Dinghies should usually be sailed bolt upright if their maximum performance is to be realized but in light winds it pays to allow some heel in order to assist the set of the sails. Boats look dramatic as they heel down under the wind but it is an inefficient way of sailing because it induces leeway. First the helmsman moves his weight outboard so that he can maintain a clear lookout ahead. He moves out to the side seat and then as the wind strength increases, onto the side decking. The crew then duplicates these moves to add extra counter-balancing weight until finally, in the strongest winds, both lean well out over the side with their feet tucked securely under the toe straps.

The helmsman must always keep a watchful eye on his destination. The wind continually swings from side to side as well as varying in strength and so the helmsman must employ all his senses to steer a correct course. Eyes first on the water looking for extra wind puffs streaking the surface, then onto the sail luff searching for any flutter and finally up to the burgee for any warning of a wind change. His cheeks will sense a

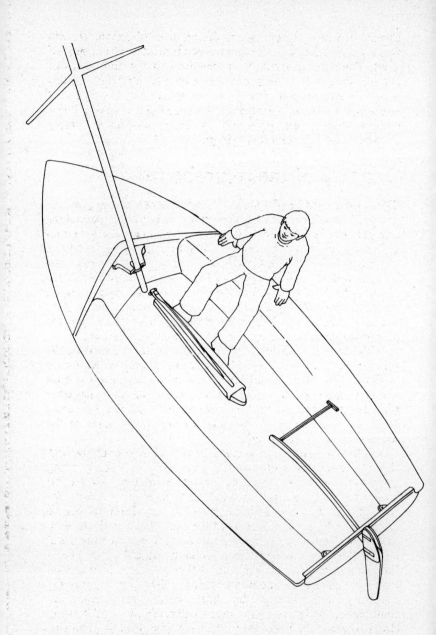

Crew positioned on the weather gunwhale at the forward part of the cockpit ready to counterbalance the heeling thrust of the wind

change in wind strength or an alteration in direction. He will also see dark ripples on the water which indicate a strong gust of wind. The natural balancing mechanisms of the body warn of changes in heeling angle or a build-up of wave strength. All this flow of information should be assessed and the required adjustments to sails, steering and balance made quickly. These natural abilities are possessed by everyone—sailing simply develops sensitivity to a very high pitch.

The role of the centreboard

The centreboard height must also be matched to the point of sailing. The adjustable centreboard not only permits launching and recovery through shallow water but also ensures maximum efficiency beneath the water. Windward sailing produces excessive leeway which can be resisted by lowering the centreboard to its full depth. This leeway is greatly reduced when sailing across the wind and so the centreboard can be raised to the halfway position in order to reduce underwater drag. Downwind produces no leeway at all and so the drag can be eliminated by raising the centreboard up inside the case.

With the wind blowing across the port side of the boat, the sails correctly sheeted (about halfway out, matching the burgee angle) and the centreboard in the half-raised position, the boat will be broad reaching under perfect control. A slight change in tiller direction to move the boat towards the wind and a sheeting in of the sails will cause the boat to sail much closer to the wind—beating close-hauled.

Ask the crew to lower the centreboard, while you gently push the tiller away for a bit and the bows will immediately swing towards the wind. At the same time tighten in both jib sheet and main sheet so that the sail angle moves nearer towards the centreline of the boat. This will ensure that the luffs will still lie asleep, matching the new angle of the wind. Instruct the crew to lower the centreboard fully in order to resist the increased leeway. The closer sail angle will probably cause the boat to heel rather more and so both crew and helmsman must be alert and ready to move their counterbalancing weight out towards the weather side. Moving the tiller away from you and simultaneously tightening the sheets will cause the boat to swing closer towards the wind. Any further adjustments beyond this point will simply start the sails shaking along their luffs: to correct this, pull the tiller across the boat towards you until the sails fill again.

A new lesson has been learned. Though luff flutter when reaching can be corrected *either* by sheeting the sails tighter *or* by altering course to bring the wind more abeam, the same options do not exist when sailing close-hauled to windwards. Here the option is limited to changing course further away from the wind. Sailing too close to the wind can be a temptation for it can offer a much more direct course towards one's final destination. It's aptly called pinching—but it drastically slows the boat's speed and so should be constantly guarded against. Sails must always be kept full and should be trimmed at the first sign of a flutter.

Tacking

Any upwind destination can only be reached by tacking from side to side in a zig-zag course. Tacking is the most basic and essential skill in sailboat control and continual practice improves even the most experienced helmsmen. Olympic helmsmen often spend hours simply practising tacking around a buoy in order to cut seconds from their time.

Switching from tack to tack is a simple manoeuvre once the technique has been learned, but many beginners often stall 'head to wind' and are then blown backwards along the course they have already travelled. The nautical phrase for this embarrassing situation is to be caught 'in irons' or 'in stays'.

The essential ingredient for successful tacking is boat speed and this can be gained by pulling the tiller towards you and simultaneously easing the sheets a little. This increases the sail loading and sets the boat sailing fast. Call out a warning 'Ready about!' and with added boat speed now assured, push the tiller firmly away across the cockpit and call out 'Lee-oh!'

The bows will swing towards the wind and at this moment it is essential to ensure that the tiller remains across the cockpit in the 'down' position. Try not to push the tiller more than 45 degrees away from the centreline, as a greater angle than this can generate stall. Once the bows of the boat have passed through the wind so that it blows from off the starboard side, the tiller can be eased back to the central position.

While all this is going on, the helmsman moves first down into the centre of the cockpit and then, as the boom swings across, out onto his new steering position on the starboard side. The move across is accomplished facing aft over the transom, for in this position it is easy to transfer the mainsheet across into the right hand and the tiller into the left. It's also prudent to keep one's head down until the boom has swung safely across onto the new tack.

The success of the tack is more assured if the crew holds the jib on the old tack until the bows have passed through the wind. Backing the jib is an old nautical trick: the deflected air flow forces the bows to swing onto the new tack. But always ensure that the crew is ready to re-set the jib on the new tack immediately the boat is pointing correctly or it will become very difficult for the helmsman to steer. Holding the jib on the old tack for too long could cause the boat to heel excessively. The crew should remain in the centre of the cockpit until the boat swings onto the new tack and then move swiftly out to the new weather side in order to counterbalance any heeling motion.

If the tack is attempted without sufficient boat speed then the helmsman will find himself 'caught in irons'. A similar result will be obtained if the rudder is centred too quickly before the tack has been completed. Keep calm. Waggling the tiller frantically from side to side will not help at all. Instruct the crew to hold the jib firmly backed onto the old tack and then as the boat begins to move backwards (to make sternway), reverse the tiller direction. This will force the bow across the wind and the boat will slowly pay off onto the desired tack.

Gybing

Tacking is a change of direction made when the bows move across the direction of the wind. When the stern moves across the direction of the wind this change of direction is called gybing.

Gybing is in one way an easy manoeuvre because there is no chance of the boat being caught in irons. When the wind blows from behind, the boom will be extended right out across the side of the boat. A gybe swings the boom across the boat from one side to the other and this can sometimes induce the most alarming rolling. In very rough weather it is quite possible that a capsize might follow a gybe and so this should first be practised in much gentler conditions.

Though the centreboard is usually in the 'up' position when

sailing downwind, it pays to lower it a fraction before a gybe in order to damp out this tendency to roll. Inform the crew of the course change by calling 'Gybe-oh!' Pull the tiller across the boat towards you and the bows will swing away from the wind. Move your weight—and your crew's weight—into the centre of the cockpit in order to keep the boat level.

As the wind moves across the stern of the boat the pressure on the mainsail will lighten, allowing the helmsman to pull in as much rope as he can handle. It will not be necessary to move the rudder. At the same time the crew grasps the boom and swings it across the boat onto the new tack. Once it has passed across the centreline the helmsman must play out the mainsheet again so that the sail moves unchecked to its new position on the other side of the boat. Both helmsman and crew—still in the centre of the cockpit—must be poised to move their weight to either side to balance any roll. As the boom swings across the boat and out onto the other side it tends to jerk the bows towards the wind. This, alas, induces roll and buries the lee side deck into the water. This is called 'broaching'. To counter this, the helmsman must move his weight out onto the new windward side and he may find it necessary to pull the tiller towards him as the boom swings over, which effectively moves the bows away from the wind. Needless to say it is essential to keep one's head down as the boom swings right across the cockpit!

Sail setting, tiller control, weight transference, tacking and gybing: these are the five basic skills which can be quite easily learned. Don't be put off by all the nautical terms and unfamiliar equipment. Sailing is very simple indeed—it just requires practice, practice, practice.

Chapter 9
Beating to windwards

Anyone can climb into a sailing dinghy and steer downwind—it's simply a question of sitting there and letting the wind blow you along. The problems and the skill are in upwind sailing—beating to windwards. Efficient windward sailing requires an ability to smell out the wind shifts and to calculate the tidal flow, and a thorough mastery of boat control. These are skills which anyone can learn but they do have to be worked for.

We have already noted that there is a natural tendency towards pinching—sailing closer and closer to the wind in order to cover a shorter course. This is self-defeating because although distance is saved, the saving is more than offset by the loss of boat speed and the added leeway made.

It is essential to have adequate forward boat speed for this generates a reciprocal head wind which in turn forms the apparent wind under which we sail. The faster our forward speed, the more this apparent wind increases and speed builds up even more. This cause and effect is very often overlooked by dinghy helmsmen as they attempt to squeeze their boats closer and closer against the wind.

Increased wind pressure on the sails adds to the heeling effect which is counterbalanced by the 'live' weight within the cockpit. Weight transference must be swift and positive if the advantage of each extra puff is to be realized—too slow and the added heel will force the lee gunwale under the water, spilling wind from the sails and causing additional drag in the water. Sitting out too long will cause the boat to heel up to windwards, dunking helmsman and crew into the water.

Extra strong puffs of wind cause the dinghy to heel sharply and so the crew must get well out over the windward side to compensate for this force. Toe straps fastened along the full length of the cockpit allow their feet to be 'anchored down' while the rest of their body weight hangs out over the side of the hull. Larger dinghies have additional aids to counter the heeling effect. Most popular is the 'trapeze' which enables the crew to hang out over the side of the boat from a wire fastened high up the mast. The lower end of this wire is hooked onto a waist-harness worn by the crew and the whole of his weight is supported by this device. Hanging from the wire, his feet braced against the outer edge of the gunwales and his body parallel to the water, he counterbalances the boat and so enables it to carry a much larger sail area.

Another similar aid is the sliding seat, though this is available on only a few boats. This is a sliding plank which fits across the mid-section of the boat and can be extended to project over the side of either gunwale. The crew, perched on the end of this plank, exerts a leverage similar to that gained with the trapeze, though the sliding seat's extra weight, cost and additional windage have prevented it from gaining general acceptance.

We have noted how the live weight within the cockpit must be moved from side to side in order to counter the heeling effects. It is also essential to distribute the weight fore and aft to minimize underwater hull drag. Underwater surfaces of the hull create skin friction which slows the boat down and the wider section aft creates much more drag than the slimmer sections forward. It is therefore important—particularly in light airs when the effects of drag are most apparent—to keep the weight well forward in order to lift the broader stern section clear of the water. In rougher weather drag is not so noticeable and the tendency is then to move aft so that stability is gained by depressing the broad stern sections into the water. Each type of boat has its own point of balance and, of course, each boat is also affected by the overall crew weight. A few experiments in weight distribution will soon determine the best positions in your boat.

Choosing a course

Steering to reach a destination directly upwind offers a wide variety of possible courses to be sailed. One could sail half the distance on port tack, turn and sail the remaining distance on starboard tack. This would be termed 'making it in two boards'—each board being the distance sailed between tacks. Another way would be to sail a quarter of the distance on port; tack and then sail another quarter on starboard; tack and a quarter distance on port, before a final tack towards one's destination. This would be getting home in four boards. A further possibility would be to make several short boards on either side of the centre line. All these courses cover precisely the same distance and theoretically each would take the same time.

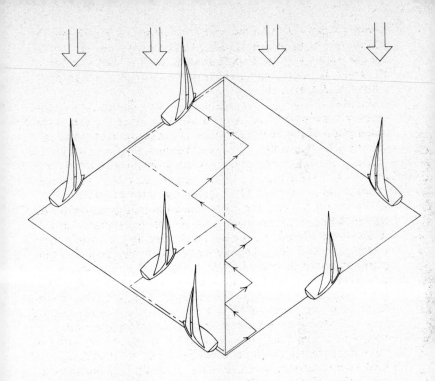

Beating to windwards. Short tacks close to the rhumb (centre) line are better than longer tacks out towards the side of the course

In fact this is not so because each time a tack is made the wind's thrust on the sails is lost and time will be wasted.

On the other hand sailing the two-board course will economize on tacking but leaves you vulnerable to sudden wind shifts which may eventually result in a longer course being sailed. It is this continual challenge of having to deal with the unexpected which makes windward sailing so rewarding.

Even a strong prevailing wind oscillates from one side to the other. In general it swings alternately from the left and from the right and so in the long run balances out. The prevailing wind direction is really an average position between the swings. The strength and timing of these shifts is always affected by the local surroundings—trees, tall buildings or hills—and the astute helmsman can steer his boat to take maximum advantage of the changes.

With the sails correctly sheeted and the boat heading to windwards, the helmsman must watch the weather conditions continually. The boat's direction must be compared constantly with both the set of the sails and the angle of the burgee—any discrepancy between their angles must be instantly corrected by a course change, alteration of sail trim or even a change onto a new tack.

A flutter along the jib luff indicates a heading wind shift. The already close-sheeted sails cannot be tightened any more to quieten this flutter and bearing away would only result in the boat sailing a longer distance. The proper action is to tack immediately because a heading wind shift on this tack means a freeing lift on the other tack and consequently a shorter course towards one's destination.

Make it a practice to move the tiller away from you a fraction every half minute or so, which will nudge the bows a little bit nearer towards the wind. If the jib luff flutters return immediately to course because the wind is still blowing from its original direction. But if the boat can be steered much nearer to the wind before the flutter starts, obviously the wind has freed and you will be able to sail a more direct course towards your destination.

By continually checking on the wind shifts and either tacking or heading up, the observant skipper can materially shorten the actual distance sailed.

Currents and tides

The problems caused by wind shifts apply equally whether you are sailing inland or at sea. But on rivers, estuaries and on the open sea there is the further problem of currents and tides to contend with. A river or an estuary poses straightforward problems concerning the current strength and the depth of water. Sailing with the current—which flows at its strongest in deep water—obviously generates extra boat speed so you should always steer for the fastest flow. The current flow is always much less in shallow water and this is the place to be when going against the current.

It may not always be possible to steer for the very best current flow as this may sometimes be shadowed by some obstruction. There is no point in choosing a favourable current flow if it is completely blanketed from the wind by a tall building or a group of trees. Again, it is a matter of experience and good judgement whether to choose a favourable current and less wind or to venture out into an adverse flow with more wind to drive you along.

There is the extra challenge of continuously changing tidal flow when you sail out at sea. Not only does it rise and fall twice a day but it also varies in strength through that six-hour cycle. The flow rate is always at its lightest during the first and sixth hour, intensifying up to its peak at about the fourth hour. These are all calculable factors which can be gleaned from the local tide tables.

Beating to windwards on port tack with a strong tide under the starboard (lee) bow will effectively push the boat faster and closer to windwards. A similar boat on starboard tack would have this tide on his port (weather) bow, which would push him down away from his destination. In this instance the port tack would be the favoured one and the starboard tack must be avoided when possible except where the tidal flow is judged to be weaker. Local charts will indicate the channels where the water flow is at its strongest.

Roll tack

With all these variables to choose from, it can be seen how important it is to assess the situation quickly and take immediate action. Usually by minimizing the adverse effects on one tack you can equally maximize the advantages on the other tack. It is therefore important to increase one's tacking speed particularly in light airs. A good technique is the roll tack. First ease the mainsheet and move inboard slightly. This causes the boat to heel momentarily to leewards. The tiller is then pushed hard down and both helmsman and crew move back to their *original* windward seating position. This causes the boat to roll violently to windwards and as the sails 'fan' across the boat onto the new tack, the helmsman and crew move smartly across to the new weather side, sheet in the sails and simultaneously jerk the heeling boat upright. The effect of this is to catapult the boat forward onto its new tack and in light airs can actually increase the speed for a few moments.

Windward sailing is a technique which can only be learned with practice. Race regularly against similar boats so that you can judge the progress you are making. Sail for specific points—don't just aimlessly drift around. Practise tacking on every wind shift, no matter how small it is, until you can spin the boat in its own length without any noticeable loss of speed. No matter what the wind direction or current strength, your prime concern is to sail the shortest distance in the shortest time. The age-old problem is whether to point high or sail fast. The best skippers somehow manage to do both.

Chapter 10
Reaching and planing

With the wind off the beam, the sails eased out over the side and wide open water to leeward, the beginner can really enjoy himself. Reaching is the fastest and easiest point of sailing and in strong winds most centreboard dinghies can be made to 'plane' on top of the waves.

There is a vastly reduced sideways thrust upon the hull, so much less leeway is made. The centreboard can therefore be partially retracted into the case reducing underwater drag. Lifting the centreboard also reduces the effect of weather helm, the heavier steering characteristics which accompany a strong beam wind. The setting of the centreboard depends upon the direction of the wind—the further aft it blows, the more the board is hoisted. The range of adjustments is of course infinite, though many owners paint lines along the centreboard to mark the quarter, half and three-quarter raised positions. It is then a simple task for the crew to make the correct adjustment to suit the wind position.

The sails must also be matched to the wind direction, being eased out more and more as the wind draws aft. The sails also react better to a beam wind if their shape is altered to provide a deeper flow curve. This can be done by slackening the outhaul tension along the boom and easing the luff tension up the mast. Many boats are now fitted with adjustable luff and foot tensioning gear which make adjustment easy during the course of sailing.

Careful sheeting of the jib is important too. Not only must a watchful eye be kept upon the luff but equal attention must also be paid to the leach. If this is sheeted too close the wind travelling across the front face of the jib cannot easily escape through the 'slot' between the jib's leach and the back of the mainsail. The width of this slot is critical: too wide and the wind speed will be insufficient; too narrow and the congested slot will divert the wind flow into the back of the mainsail. If this happens the mainsail will lift and shake along the luff and its efficiency will be ruined. This is called back-winding.

There is considerably less heeling force when the wind is off the beam, and boat balance is much easier to maintain. Usually it is sufficient for the helmsman to be seated out on the side deck with the crew inside the cockpit. Both must be alert to move their weight quickly to match a change in the wind's strength, for dinghies will not reach fast when heeled. Once a boat starts to heel the underwater balance is disturbed, the lee side of the hull becoming much more deeply immersed and thus generating extra drag. This lee side drag causes the bows of the boat to swerve up quickly to windwards and this in turn creates even more heel which may eventually result in a capsize. Be ready to guard against this by rapid transfer of weight coupled with an easing of the sails to meet an extra heavy puff of wind.

It is possible to reach towards any chosen destination without tacking, though it is advisable to make small allowances for cross tides or wind shifts. Steer just a few points upwind so that any of these adverse conditions can be offset without having to make major course corrections at the end of the journey. If you overcorrect, then, apart from a slight loss of speed, nothing is lost by bearing away a little and either broad reaching or running down to your destination.

We have already seen how the true wind and the reciprocal wind combine to form the apparent sailing wind. Reaching dinghies can move fast enough to generate very high apparent wind speeds, which move further and further forward of the beam as the speed builds up. It is therefore necessary to be continually adjusting the sheeting angle to match the wind direction in order to obtain the maximum performance. Catamarans and some very fast dinghies build up such a high reaching speed that their sails finally have to be trimmed to the close-hauled position.

Planing is the ultimate thrill, for under sufficient wind strength the boat will lift up and skim across the surface of the water at several times its displacement speed. Normally boat speed is limited by the waterline length, because all boats travel within a trough formed by their bow and stern waves. Increasing their power only serves to build up these two waves so they sink deeper into the trough. Thus the speed of displacement can be calculated by the formula $\sqrt{\text{waterline length}} \times 1.25 = \text{speed in knots}$.

Light-weight planing dinghies do not suffer from these limitations, for their carefully shaped hulls, driven by powerful sails, enable them to climb up onto the bow wave and the cycle is broken. Once clear of the trough the boat's wetted area is vastly reduced and the lessened skin friction enables it to travel even faster. Planing is superbly exciting and, providing the boat is kept bolt upright, a high degree of stability can be easily maintained.

It is the harder puffs of wind which set a dinghy planing and the helmsman should keep a watchful eye for these moving towards him. They usually show themselves as dark rippled patches along the surface and are known descriptively as 'cat's paws'. Tighten in the sheets just a fraction before the gust arrives and pull up the helm a little. This action turns the boat away from the wind and encourages it to skid away under the wind's impact. In contrast, keeping the boat on course or heading up a little will invite the gust to force the hull deeper into the water and destroy all hope of planing.

As the gust strikes, both helmsman and crew should move their weight outboard to counterbalance and move back in the cockpit in order to lift the bows onto the bow wave. With the bows out of the water, the boat settles down onto the broader sections aft and on this stable platform the boat skims across the water rather like a flat bouncing pebble. The increased speed will immediately bring the apparent wind forward causing the sail luffs to flutter. Rather than tightening in the sheets it is better to pull the tiller towards you a fraction and refill the sails. This action keeps the boat in contact with the wind gust which is moving away downwind and prolongs the plane.

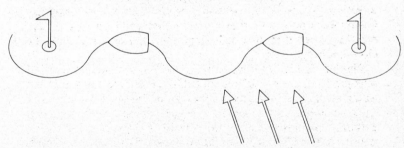

Playing the wind puffs on a reaching leg. Bear away in the harder gusts and luff up in the lulls in order to maintain maximum boat speed

As the gust fades, push away the tiller and tighten in the sheets. This course of action builds up the apparent wind speed again and keeps the boat moving fast. It also brings the boat back onto the original direction which was lost when planing downwind. The rule for sailing downwind in planing conditions is always to bear away in the puffs and luff up in the lulls.

Firm, positive rudder control is of great importance for successful downwind reaching. If the rudder blade is held down by a shockcord under tension then the high-speed surge of water may overcome its tension and cause it to pivot upwards. If this happens severe weather helm will develop immediately, making the boat difficult to steer. The bows will turn to windwards and either a capsize will result or the rudder blade might snap. It is therefore preferable to hold the rudder blade down with either a wire or a permanent locking clamp rather than the more customary shockcord.

A correctly planing dinghy always leaves a smooth flat wake streaming out behind the transom. A spume of spray fountaining out of this wake indicates that too much rudder control is being needed to steer the boat. Effective correction can usually be made by lifting the centreboard a little, moving the crew weight further aft in the cockpit and ensuring that the rudder blade is in its fully down position. Check that the sails are correctly eased out to meet the wind direction. Over-sheeting will also generate excessive heel and weather helm. Always try to keep the boat flat, and the mast bolt upright. A good visual aid is to maintain a mental picture of the hull directly beneath the mast and sails. Never let the top of the mast be out over one side or the other of the cockpit.

Chapter 11
Running free

Downwind courses always seem to be the easiest ones to sail, a time to sit back and let the wind blow you where it will. But just as in beating and reaching, it takes all the helmsman's concentration to get the best out of his boat.

It is noticeable that boats bunch together when sailing downwind because their sails blanket the wind from each other. Crisp boat handling plus maximum sailing speed are the remedies for breaking clear of the pack into open wind.

Ease onto the run from the broad reach by pulling up the tiller and, at the same time, allowing the mainsail to run out until the boom rests against the shrouds. The boat will turn away from the broad reach until the wind is blowing from astern—running free. If the wind is blowing strongly, the added pressure will force the boom hard against the lee shroud. This unfortunately moves the top part of the mainsail forward of the mast and so upsets the steering balance of the boat. This can be prevented simply by tying a stopknot in the mainsheet, which will then jam against the transom block when the boom has reached its optimum outward swing. It is a good idea to tie this stopknot in the mainsheet before going afloat so that the correct position can be found.

Leeway is not a factor to be considered when running free because the wind's thrust is directly down the fore and aft line of the boat. The centreboard can therefore be raised up into the case, eliminating all underwater drag from this source. In light airs it is possible to raise the rudder blade as well, reducing the wetted areas to a minimum. If you raise the rudder blade in light airs you gain more control over the steering which otherwise tends to be insensitive. In windy conditions it is wise to lower the centreboard a bit to damp-out any rolling tendencies. The rudder must always be fully lowered in wind, otherwise the exaggerated 'feel' will develop into weather helm and could result in a capsize or a broken rudder.

Rolling from side to side is very unpleasant and if allowed to continue unchecked, may capsize the boat. Positioning the crew correctly guards against this. It is caused by the wind thrusting hard against the mainsail when it is extended over the side of the

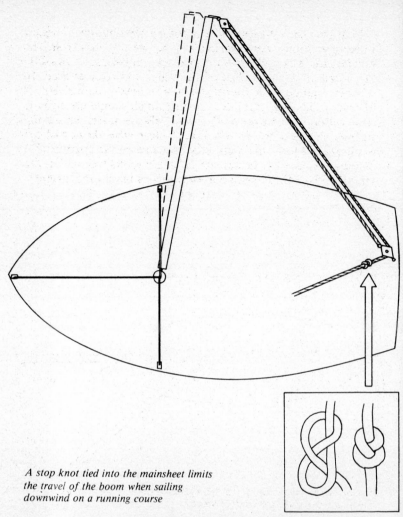

A stop knot tied into the mainsheet limits the travel of the boom when sailing downwind on a running course

boat without anything to balance the thrust. Setting the jib on the opposite side of the boat ('goose-winging') is advantageous when running before the wind and also helps to reduce any rolling. The jib can be held out in the goose-winged position either by the crew or, even better, by a jib stick or 'whisker pole'. This pole has a slim spike at one end and an open hook at the other. The spike is pushed into the metal cringle at the clew of the jib and the hook clipped onto an eye fastened onto the front of the mast. The crew should keep his weight as low in the cockpit as possible to avoid further rolling.

Boat balance is critical and the correct distribution of weight will also go a long way towards damping out any lateral roll. The weight should be well forward in most conditions, as this lifts the broad aft sections clear of the water and reduces drag. In rougher conditions the weight should be moved progressively aft in order to improve stability. The helmsman should arrange the crew within the cockpit so that he is always seated up on the weather side deck where he can get a clear view ahead past the goose-winged jib. Usually the crew is seated on the opposite side of the cockpit where he can act as a counterbalance and at the same time hold the boom out at right angles against the shroud.

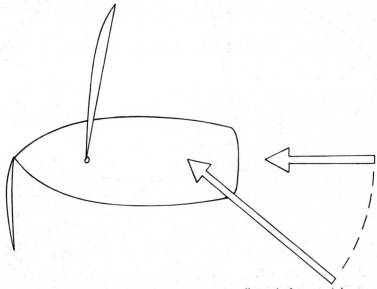

Running free. Wind is always kept on quarter to allow a 'safety margin' should there be a windshift across the stern

Try to sail downwind courses with the wind blowing from over the weather corner of the transom rather than from dead astern. With the wind over the weather quarter, there is a safety margin available should there be a sudden wind shift. If the wind was blowing from dead behind then a sudden leeward shift would move the wind around behind the mainsail causing it to slam across the boat in a 'gybe all standing'. These unexpected gybes can be very dangerous, for the tremendous force of the mainsail and boom slamming across the cockpit can put severe strain on all the rigging and may cause an immediate capsize. There is also a strong possibility that unwary heads might receive a severe blow.

When the wind does manage to get around the 'wrong side' of the mainsail it is termed 'sailing by the lee'. Even if an involuntary gybe does not result immediately, it is still wrong to continue sailing by the lee because the efficiency of the sails is much reduced. Guard against this by keeping a constant eye on the wind's direction and making alterations in the steering to keep it on the weather quarter. In fact, all downwind runs are sailed as very broad reaches.

Gybing

If it is impossible to keep adjusting the steering in order to keep the wind on the quarter then you must move the sails across onto the other side. Most newcomers to sailing are unduly anxious about the problems of gybing mainly because they have been influenced by comments from other sailors. Gybing does have its problems but so do tacking, planing and coming ashore. The key to success is confidence. In many ways gybing can be much easier than tacking for there is certainly no danger about becoming caught in irons.

It is easier to gybe when the wind is blowing either at a constant speed or its maximum speed. Do not gybe in sudden lulls or at moments when the wind speed is picking up again. The reason for this is quite simple: the constant pressure of the wind upon the sails reduces the actual wind speed against the boat. For example, if the wind is blowing at 10 knots and the boat is travelling at 6 knots then the pressure upon the sails is only 4 knots and it is easy to swing the boom across the boat. But if the boat momentarily slows down to only 2 knots then the pressure against the sails rises to 8 knots, making it much harder to swing the boom across. The extra effort required to heave the boom across against this pressure may well start the boat rolling with the usually inevitable result. Capsize!

Successful gybing can best be accomplished by establishing a set routine and sticking to it. It might well be described as gybing by numbers.

1   Warn the crew of the impending change of course.
2   The crew removes the jib stick from the jib and stows it safely away.

3   Pull the tiller up in order to swing the bows away from the wind. This allows the wind to move across the transom and blow from the reverse side of the mainsail. It also reduces the wind pressure on the mainsail and makes it easier to pull the boom across.

4   Take in less than a metre of mainsheet so that the boom moves inboard a little. This should be quite easy because of the lowered wind pressure upon the sail. If there is excessive pressure make further steering adjustments so that the wind moves even further around the sail. Never force the pace—once the boat has been correctly set up it will virtually gybe itself.

5   Hold the tiller straight.

6   This is the moment to gybe!

7   Helmsman and crew move into the centre of the cockpit, keeping their heads low and ready to counterbalance any roll.

8   The helmsman gives the action call 'Gybe-oh!' and immediately starts hauling in on the mainsheet.

9   The crew grasps hold of the boom (or sometimes the kicking strap wire) and pulls the boom and mainsail across the cockpit. For the moment he ignores the jib, for the prime consideration is to get the mainsail correctly set on the other side of the boat.

10 Once the boom and mainsail have crossed the centreline of the cockpit the mainsheet must be rapidly paid out to ease it on its way. This paying out of the mainsheet slows just before the boom completes its journey, otherwise it will slam against the lee shroud.

11 A small amount of reverse tiller action is needed just before the boom completes its journey to counter any tendency for the bows to broach up into wind.

12 Both crew and helmsman should still be poised ready to move out windwards to counterbalance any heel to leewards.

13 Once the boat is stable and safely onto its new course, the helmsman and crew should resume their normal positions and the jib stick replaced in the goose-winged position.

Gybing around an obstruction

This is gybing on a dead run occasioned by a progressive wind shift to leewards. It is sometimes necessary to gybe around an obstruction such as a moored buoy, a headland or a bend in the river. In this case it is quite likely that you will approach the gybe point on something of a broad reach, bear momentarily away onto a dead run and then, once the gybe has been completed, harden up into a new reach on the other tack. The technique, however, is exactly the same as described above except that you

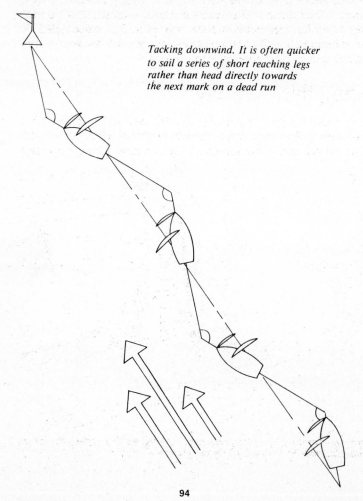

Tacking downwind. It is often quicker to sail a series of short reaching legs rather than head directly towards the next mark on a dead run

should remember first to haul up the centreboard before commencing the gybe and of course to lower it again once the new reach is commenced. It is essential to gybe around an obstruction with the centreboard fully raised so that the hull can skid sideways on the water, dissipating the force generated by the fast swinging boom and sail.

Downwind sailing is generally slower than reaching because the boat is continuously moving away from the wind. Extra speed can be built up by broad reaching towards one side of the running course and then gybing in order to broad reach towards the other side. This technique is called 'tacking downwind' and substantially increases the boat's speed through the water. Of course it does mean that an extra distance is sailed, so a balance must be maintained between speed gained and distance sailed. A few experiments will soon reveal the amount of distance which can be sacrificed economically to speed.

Using the spinnaker

Many small dinghies are equipped with a spinnaker to aid them when sailing downwind and, though they were once considered to be purely racing equipment, they are now found on many

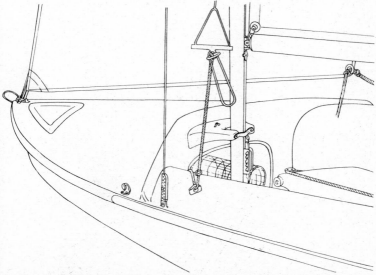

More sophisticated gear. Trapeze handles and hook-up rings; spinnaker chute; multi-adjustable jib tensioning lever on lower face of mast

family cruising boats. The spinnaker is a light-weight nylon sail, spherical in shape, which is set out in front of the forestay so that it collects most of the following wind. Its area often equals the total area of both the mainsail and the jib. It adds substantially to the boat's performance and skilled crews often use it on reaching courses as well as those downwind. Remember that as it is cut from light-weight cloth, it is fragile and easily torn.

The spinnaker is hoisted and lowered whilst afloat and is controlled by two sheets which lead from each of its bottom corners back through fairleads on the side decks. When not in use it is stowed either in special bags beneath the foredeck or, in more recent designs, inside a circular tube which emerges close by the bows. This tube is called a spinnaker chute and enables this sail to be hoisted and lowered quickly to suit the wind conditions.

Once the spinnaker has been hoisted, it is held out in position by a long pole which fastens onto the bottom corner of the sail and the forward side of the mast, very much like the jib stick.

Spinnakers should not be handled by beginners because the complexities caused by continually having to hoist and lower the sail can create tangles in the rigging. Concentrate all your efforts on the mainsail and the jib until sail handling becomes second nature. Only then should you divert your attentions to the fascinations of spinnaker work.

Chapter 12
Dealing with trouble

Beginners are usually wise enough to confine their early sailing days to sunny pleasant conditions with just a light breeze blowing into their sails. Beginners should not stray too far from land as it is not possible always to regulate the weather. So it is important to acquire quickly the skill needed to tame the squally conditions which are so much a feature of our climate.

Strong winds

The effect of stronger winds is immediately noticed when beating to windwards. The boat heels more, extra leeway is made and the lee gunwale may even scoop beneath the water bringing litres of water into the cockpit. All these conditions can be avoided if the helmsman and crew are ready to deal with them. Indeed, strong winds can be turned into a positive asset.

Both helmsman and crew should be seated out on the side deck, feet under the toe straps, and ready to move their combined weight further over the side to counterbalance the wind's thrust. The helmsman should be scanning the water constantly to windwards, looking for the telltale ripples heralding that extra-hard gust. Then—just before the gust strikes—both should shift their weight outboard so that the boat is held bolt upright. Waiting until the gust strikes before moving outboard is no good because once the boat has been allowed to heel it becomes very much harder to haul it upright again. (It helps to have adjustable toe straps so that their length can be modified to suit individual leg lengths.)

Sometimes an extra-hard gust strikes with such force that weight transference is insufficient to keep the boat upright. In this case the mainsheet must be quickly eased out so that the mainsail is presented at a wider angle to the wind. Once the gust has spilled from the sail it can be trimmed in again to its original setting. The jib should not be eased except in the direst emergency when a 'knock-down' squall dictates that everything should be let go.

Both the methods described deal with extra-hard gusts in a crude way, for the boat tends to progress in a series of jerks. A more sophisticated technique is to blend the rapid sail adjustments, the weight transfer and sensitive tiller control into a continual pattern which exploits each wind variation to maximum advantage. Experienced helmsmen and crew sit out with each gust, trim the sails to suit and ease the tiller away a fraction in order to steer the boat closer to the wind. This last action reduces the wind loading on the sail and allows a more direct course to windwards to be steered. Once the gust has passed the sails are retrimmed, the weight moved inboard and the original course resumed. This luff-and-bear-away technique requires lots of practice but once perfected it allows excellent windward progress to be made. Great care must be taken to resume course once the gust has passed, otherwise a following gust will catch the boat in irons.

Running before a high wind

Running before a high wind is nothing like as pleasant as planing on a reach and few helmsmen enjoy the experience. Yet it is a point of sailing which often occurs and a technique must be developed which will cope with the problems. Strong following winds produce alarming rolls, with the boom flying first into the air and then down into the water. Once this roll develops, the boom will dig deeper and deeper into the water until the drag will trip the boat and a capsize may follow.

A balanced weight distribution does much to reduce this rolling and helmsman and crew should be seated out on opposing side decks, helmsman to weather and crew to leeward. As the wind strength increases they should move further back towards the transom in order to stabilize the boat on the broad aft sections. Lowering the centreboard about one-third also helps to damp out these rolls. The wind pressures can be equalized to some extent by goose-winging the jib firmly and the crew, keeping low, should make every effort to fix the jib stick in position.

Reefing

It is foolhardy to go afloat in wind strengths beyond one's capabilities though, of course, it is essential to gain experience in these conditions. A compromise can be reached by reducing the total sail area before going afloat by taking in a reef. Many small dinghies are equipped with reefing points along the sail or the more modern roller-reefing system.

Reefing points

Spaced along the mainsail about 30 centimetres above the boom may be a row of small holes punched along the sail. On some sails a row of short cords dangle from these points. The mainsail is reefed down by first uncleating the halyard and lowering the mainsail about 30 centimetres down the mast. The halyard is then re-cleated and the new tack and clew point made secure. A thin line is then fed through the reefing points and around the boom lashing the excess sailcloth out of the way. Alternatively the short cords are used to lash the sail around the boom. The halyard is re-tensioned if necessary and the mainsail, in its reduced size, is ready. Some sails have several rows of reefing points each about 30 centimetres above the other so that the sail can be reduced progressively to meet stormier conditions.

It is important that the boat should first be turned head to wind before the sail is reefed so that the weight of the wind on the sail is reduced thus making the sail easier to handle.

Roller reefing

Roller reefing can best be described step-by-step:

1   First remove the kicking strap wire from its keyhole slot beneath the boom.
2   Uncleat the main halyard and lower the mainsail about 30 centimetres. Re-cleat the halyard.
3   Pull the boom away from the squared shank of the gooseneck until the boom can be revolved.
4   Wind the lowered mainsail cloth around the boom, taking care to ensure that the creases in the sail are smoothed out by hand as the boom revolves.
5   The mainsail can be progressively reduced in size by simply lowering more down the mast and winding the excess around the boom, but make sure that the bottom batten is first removed from its pocket.
6   Refix the boom onto the gooseneck and tension the main halyard.
7   Finally, check that the mainsheet and block on the end of the boom have not become entangled during the furling operation.

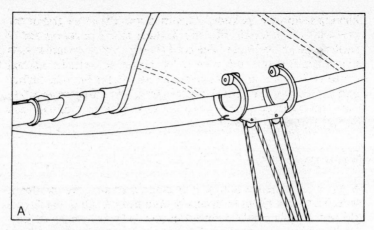

Reefing devices. a) Reefing claw. b) Knotted rope inserted into kicking strap eye and then furled with sail

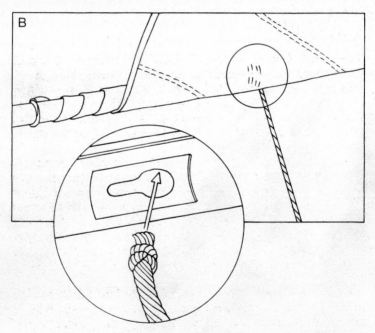

It is advisable to rig up some form of temporary kicking strap gear for it can be dangerous to sail in high winds without one. One good way is to fasten a length of line to one end of the kicking strap wire. A knot is then tied into the other end of the line which is inserted into the keyhole slot before the sail is furled around the boom. The cord thus becomes wound in with the sail and allows the wire to be tensioned with its normal controls. It is not as effective as the usual gear but will suffice under a reduced sail plan. An alternative is to purchase a reefing claw which can be hooked onto the kicking strap wire and then clamped around the furled sail.

Storm sails

A more permanent solution is to hoist a smaller suit of storm sails. These can either be specially obtained or, alternatively, an old suit of sails can be reduced in size for you by a sailmaker. Another idea is to obtain a cheap secondhand suit of sails from the owner of a much smaller dinghy.

Capsize!

There are many thousands of sailors who have yet to capsize even though they have been at the helm for years. Though this may be a tribute to their skill or luck, it is more likely that they choose only to go afloat in calm conditions. Whatever the reason, it is certain that they now have an exaggerated fear of capsizing and they might well prove to be seriously at risk should disaster ever overtake them.

Many will say that capsizing is a result of poor seamanship and in some instances this is true. But the unexpected can—and does—often occur and every small boat crew should be trained to deal with it. Fear of capsizing is much worse than the event itself and so practice on a warm, sunny day will soon dispel any worries on this score. Once you are able to right the boat yourself swiftly and easily the problem ceases to exist. Every sailing school teaches easy methods of recovering from a capsize.

Capsizing happens in two ways. Either the boat will heel so far to leeward that the scooped-in water drags it over on its side, or the wind momentarily stops, dropping the stretched out crewmen into the water. Both eventualities should be avoided by taking the steering and sheeting precautions described on pages 79-80. Even so, an unexpected wind change can catch even the most experienced crews unawares.

A rescue team may miss a dark head swimming in the water but they can easily spot an upturned boat. Racing fleets usually have at least one rescue boat in attendance, but remember that their assistance disqualifies you from further participation in that race.

The leeward capsize is the easiest to deal with. It usually happens quite slowly, leaving the mast and sail floating flat on the water with skipper and crew perched on the upturned gunwale. It is then easy for them to step over the side onto the centreboard, hook their hands beneath the side decking and haul the boat upright. Take good care to stand very close to the hull where the centreboard emerges through the slot. This will not give as much leverage as that gained by standing further out along the centreboard but it reduces the danger of snapping it in two! If you are both heavy-weights then it is better if only one of you stands on the centreboard.

If the boat has swung round down the wind there is some danger of the boat coming upright too fast and re-capsizing on the other side. It is therefore a good idea for the crew to swim out to the bows and hold the boat firmly into the wind. Try always to swing the boat around so that when lying flat on the water, the hull is to windward of the rig.

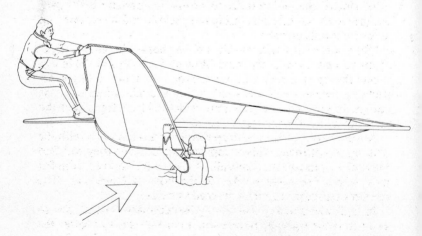

Capsize. Helmsman stands on centreboard and heaves boat upright using the jib sheets for leverage. Crew remains at bow keeping boat headed towards the wind

Usually the man on the centreboard can scramble back inboard as the boat comes upright. He can then sort out the gear and start bailing out the water. The other crewman can swim down to the transom where he can hold the rudder and thus steer the boat into wind. This is important, for if the wind comes round onto the beam then the stationary boat could easily be knocked down again. It is also very much easier for him to climb back in over the transom than over the much higher gunwale. In any case climbing over the gunwale is apt to induce a capsize.

Violent leeward capsizes may catapult the crew off the side deck and onto the sail. This additional weight will almost certainly force the sail under the water and cause the boat to roll upside down or 'turn turtle' which makes recovery more difficult.

Helmsman and crew should station themselves on opposite sides of the upturned hull. The crew throws one of the jib sheets to the helmsman waiting on the other side. It is picked up by the helmsman and, with his feet braced against the gunwale, he extends his body to full stretch. This leverage is usually sufficient to roll the boat over onto its side but in extreme conditions his partner may have to swim round and add his weight to the rope.

Once the boat is on its side, the crew must place himself on the other side of the hull in order to steady its upward rush. Light-weight crews can often lie inside the cockpit and be scooped up as the boat rolls upright.

Make sure that when you do start to heave the boat upright again you do so with the wind blowing into the sail. This will steady the upward rush and prevent the boat from rolling over. Righting the boat with the wind behind the sail swings the boat upright in an ever-quickening arc which will continue past the vertical into another certain capsize.

A windward capsize will drop the crew into the water with the boat on top of them. This is unpleasant, for often they will find themselves beneath the mainsail. It is essential to keep calm for it is only a few short strokes to the boat and open air. The recovery technique can then proceed as before.

In high winds or big seas it may be necessary for the crew to swim into the cockpit, release the main halyard and lower the sail. Sometimes the halyard may become entangled and may prevent the sail from being lowered. In this case the crew must swim out to the masthead and unshackle the sail so that it can be lowered. Remember that when the boat comes upright again it will be impossible to rehoist the mainsail because the halyard will be still up at the masthead. It is important therefore to free the halyard and pull the end back to the foot of the mast so the sail can eventually be rehoisted.

Adequate buoyancy is of course essential. If there is too little, the boat will float hopelessly low in the water, often with most of the stern and mid-sections totally submerged. Too much buoyancy is equally dangerous for it allows the hull to float so high that the crew cannot climb back inboard again. It also causes excess windage and the boat may float away downwind from the swimming crew.

The need to be a competent swimmer has already been emphasized. Non-swimmers should not venture out. However, aided by a first-class life-jacket, even a non-swimmer could carry out the recovery procedures described. Under no circumstances should anyone ever leave the boat in an attempt to swim to shore—even if the boat cannot be righted they may well find the distance beyond their swimming ability.

Check on the safety and well-being of your crew immediately after the capsize. The helmsman tends to be fully occupied during a capsize and he may overlook what is happening elsewhere. Make sure also that everyone is back on board and that those who have been immersed in the water for some time are not suffering from exposure.

If you are spending a day cruising, tell someone on shore where you are going and what time you hope to return. Then if you do meet trouble the rescue team will know where to look for you. Prevention is always much better than cure.

How to take a tow

Take the towline first around the forestay and then make it fast to the mast or around the thwart. Lower the sails and maintain rudder control so that you are towed bows first in line with the rescue boat. Never be towed sideways or upside down for this may cause severe damage. Always keep a large plastic bucket aboard and make sure that it is firmly tied down. Put the attachment line through a hole drilled into the top of the bucket—handles have been known to come off! A boat full of water can weigh a tonne or more and is difficult to tow. Each bucketful dumped over the side lightens the load and lifts the hull higher out of the water. A small plastic scoop and a sponge.

will dispose of the final bilge water. Automatic bailers can be fitted which suck the water out but the boat needs to be travelling at some speed for these to work effectively. Bailers work at their best when the boat has only a little bilge water and is travelling fast on a broad reach under full sail. They are usually found only on racing boats.

Chapter 13
On the racing scene

Beginners are often reluctant to join in club racing, feeling that their lack of knowledge may well spoil other people's pleasure. These misgivings are reinforced by just one glance at the complicated rule book and then finally confirmed by the shouts of 'Starboard!' and 'Water!' which they hear in every race. In fact, these fears are all quite unjustified, for newcomers to the racing scene are made welcome and more experienced members are always ready to explain the basic racing rules.

Although the rules do fill a book totalling sixty-eight pages (obtainable from the RYA, ref. YR1), the relevant sections affecting a beginner are explained in under twelve pages. These rules are further sub-divided into one section of 'right of way' rules which must always be obeyed and a remaining section of tactical rules which the more experienced sailor can use to turn a situation to his advantage. Learning the rules in the first part is quick and easy and will enable a beginner to start racing without running into trouble. As he progresses, he can study the ramifications of the tactical rules and gradually put his expanding knowledge into practice.

Rule 36 is the most important rule for it clearly defines which boat shall have right of way. It states that 'a port tack yacht shall at all times keep clear of a starboard tack yacht'. This means that if your boat is sailing a course with the wind blowing from over the port side of the hull (the sails eased out over the starboard side), you must keep clear of all other boats converging on a starboard tack. This rule is effective no matter whether you are beating, reaching or running. It is the fundamental rule of racing. Hence those loud shouts of 'Starboard!': they are simply warning calls from right-of-way yachts advising port tack boats to keep clear.

If the port tack yacht fails to keep clear, and either a collision occurs or the right-of-way yacht has to make a sudden last minute course change, then the defaulting boat must be penalized. Retirement from the race used to be the sole penalty but in recent years a series of graduated penalties have been introduced. It is now usual for the defaulting boat to atone by making two complete turns—the 720 degree spin—before being allowed to continue in the race.

Racing courses are laid around moored buoys, each of which has to be passed in a specified order and on one particular side. The penalty for touching one of these buoys during the rounding is to circle it again. During this recircling manoeuvre great care must be taken not to impede the progress of other boats rounding the mark for the first time.

When two or more boats approach a mark together then the boat inside must be given sufficient sailing room to get past without touching the mark. He claims this inside 'overlap' by calling 'Water!' at least two full boats' lengths before the mark is reached. This water call will only be accepted if the bows of his boat overlap the aftermost part of the boat in front, and is only valid on windward legs of the course if both boats are on the same tack; on opposing tacks the port/starboard rule 36 applies. On downwind legs water can be claimed no matter what tack is being sailed.

Another rule to learn immediately is rule 37 which is sub-divided into three short sections. Rule 37.1 states that 'a boat to windward shall keep clear of a boat to leeward'. This is obviously fair for the boat sailing up in clear wind could otherwise bear down on the defenceless leeward boat sailing in the wind shadow of its sails.

Rule 37.2: 'The boat clear astern shall keep clear of the boat clear ahead.' Again a self-explanatory rule, for an overtaking boat with a following wind would quickly shadow the one ahead and so make it impossible for it to keep out of the way.

Rule 37.3: 'A yacht which establishes an overlap to leeward from clear astern shall allow the windward yacht ample room and opportunity to keep clear and during the existence of that overlap the leeward yacht shall not sail above her proper course.' This sounds complicated and involved at first reading but closer study reveals the basic sense. Because under rules 37.1 and 37.2 the leeward yacht is protected from an attacking windward yacht a situation could develop where a leeward yacht might unfairly exploit these rules. Rule 37.3 prevents this since it prevents a leeward yacht from sailing into a 'safe' attacking position without giving the windward yacht time to get clear. Read the rule slowly again and you will begin to appreciate why sailboat racing is so often called 'chess on water'.

It should be noted that these rules apply only if both boats are on the same tack. If the overtaking boat is on a starboard tack then rule 36 applies and the defending boat must quickly get clear—or gybe over onto starboard tack as well.

If an overtaking boat does attempt to sail closely by on the weather side, as prohibited in rule 37.1, then the leeward boat may defend his position by mounting a 'luffing' attack. This is covered under rule 38 which permits the defending boat to steer a sharp course up to windwards with the intention of striking a glancing blow alongside the attacker. It is the only time when contact between the boats is sanctioned by the rules. If contact is made then the windward boat must either retire from the race or perform the two compulsory circles—each sailing club decides which type of penalty is to be employed. The leeward boat must curtail his luff once the windward boat draws ahead to a position where its helmsman, seated in his normal position, is level with the leeward boat's mast. The overtaking skipper then hails 'Mast abeam!' and the leeward boat must immediately revert to her original course.

These few basic rules will get you into club racing where further experience can be gained. Racing teaches a beginner to keep a close watch around him and split-second boat handling quickly becomes second nature. Very soon the intricacies of the tactical rules become apparent and in turn each one can be brought into play. Thus the climb up the racing ladder begins.

There will be times when over-enthusiasm or lack of skill will cause the newcomer to overstep the mark and one of the penalties already mentioned will be incurred. But there may also be times when some doubt arises about just who is at fault and neither boat feels obliged to accept the blame. In this case a protest flag—usually a handkerchief knotted in the shrouds will do—is flown and a written report given to the race officer once the race has finished. Fellow club members are asked then to form a small protest committee and consider the evidence produced by both sides, a procedure which usually results in one party being exonerated and the other disqualified from the race. These meetings are mostly good-humoured affairs which have the double purpose of quickly resolving personal disagreements and also of clarifying disputed rules. It is most important that all racing rules are scrupulously obeyed, otherwise everyone's fun is spoiled.

The most popular sort of competition is class racing. Here boats of identical design and performance compete together, starting and finishing around an agreed course. It is the fairest and most interesting type of racing, for the first boat home across the finishing line is obviously the winner.

But often there are many different types of boat within one club and it is not possible for them to race together on level terms. A handicap system has therefore been developed called the Portsmouth Yardstick Ratings and by using a few simple calculations the race officer can make allowances for the differing performances. The boats all start at the same time and race the same distance over an agreed course. Each boat's finishing time is then noted as it crosses the line and this is subtracted from the starting time. This produces an 'elapsed time'—the actual duration of the boat's own race. Obviously large, fast boats will have a short elapsed time and slower boats will take much longer. Each boat has its own Yardstick number—fast boats a low number, slower boats a higher one. By applying these Yardstick numbers to the elapsed time the race officer can quickly produce a 'corrected' time which makes due allowance for the boat's performance. Often a high Yardstick number will make a slow boat the winner on handicap even though it might have finished a long time after the actual race leader. The secret of successful handicap racing is to try to sail a little faster than the allowance given by the Yardstick rating.

There are summer regattas in most clubs, which are light-hearted affairs. Open meetings are also popular as they attract visiting helmsmen from other nearby clubs and often become highly competitive events. Keen helmsmen look forward each year to the national championships in which they can compete for the honour of becoming the class champion. These championships are usually held on the open sea and last for a whole week. As they are mostly centred on a popular holiday resort, they become a combined championship and holiday for the entire family. With this in mind, the organizers make sure that there is an extensive social programme as well.

Sailing clubs are organized by the members, most of whom give up some of their spare time to help run the club. A beginner interested in administration could start by acting as the race officer's assistant and might later lend a hand with the rescue team. As his experience grows his responsibility increases until eventually he becomes Officer of the Day for one weekend. In this capacity he is responsible for the entire running of the club and the racing. Many sailors become fascinated by this work and often forsake helming completely. Some even extend their horizons and spend their spare time acting as race officer for the bigger open meetings and national championships.

Chapter 14
Racing to win

Nearly everyone enjoys club racing. The excitement and the fun gained from racing in close quarters is magnified further by the joy in scoring a victory against an old rival at the back of the fleet. In time even winning becomes a distinct possibility. Indeed, sailors who learn how to make good starts, keep out of trouble, handle the boat competently and complete the course without gear failure should regularly finish well placed in the fleet.

Study the sailing instructions before going afloat. These detail any alterations which the local club might have made to international racing rules and give information about the courses to be sailed and the starting time of each race. They also make it clear whether penalties for rule infringement will be disqualification or the lesser 720 degree turn.

Open-sea courses are mostly sailed around three moored buoys set in a triangular course, usually with legs of about one and a half kilometres between each buoy. It is important to find out whether these marks will be rounded to port or to starboard and where both the starting and finishing lines will be placed. Inland courses can be more complicated because the restricted water requires more buoys in order to build up a sufficiently long lap. An intricate course around these marks, leaving some to port and others to starboard, is the usual arrangement and it is important to make detailed notes of the correct order before going afloat.

Leave plenty of time before each race to rig the boat, check the gear and get changed into sailing clothing. There is often a last-minute rush to get afloat and a queue of boats all waiting to launch down a narrow slipway could result in missing the start of a race. Make a point of always getting afloat early to avoid these jams and then use the time gained to check the wind's strength and direction and to make a few practice starts.

The starting line cannot be painted onto the water and it is therefore indicated by two markers at each end of the line. These might be two moored boats or buoys or, for an inland race, two poles fixed on the shoreline. A series of warning signals, each exactly five minutes apart are then given, so that the competitors can time their approach to the line.

Each class of boat is given a code flag, details of which will be printed in the sailing instructions. They are based on an international code of flags, each one representing a letter of the alphabet, which enable messages to be signalled from ship to ship. Exactly ten minutes before the advertised starting time the class flag will be hoisted up the starting line flagstaff and a warning signal will be sounded. Five minutes later the Blue Peter, a blue flag superimposed with a smaller white rectangle, is hoisted to join the class flag and another sound signal is given. From this moment, everyone is under starter's orders and subject to all the racing rules. Exactly at the advertised starting time, both flags are lowered and a third sound signal made. The race is on! Remember that it is the dropping of the flags which start the race—the sound signal only draws attention to this fact and is not in itself the valid starting signal. Don't overshoot the line before the starting signal is given, otherwise you will have to go back to the starting line again.

Good starting lines are carefully positioned so that the first leg of the course will be a beat to windwards. This enables the more skillful helmsmen to break clear of the pack by using their superior tacking skills. Downwind starts usually result in a log-jam of boats piling up around the first mark.

There are few starting lines laid exactly at the right angle and one end tends to be more favoured than the other. It is possible to find out which is the favoured end by reaching up and down the length of the line before the start with the sails correctly set for a broad reach. If the starboard end is favoured then it will be possible to sail down the line on a very broad starboard reach but only possible to return on port close-hauled. A port bias works conversely of course. If neither track offers an appreciable advantage then the line is indeed set squarely to the wind.

Always approach the line on starboard tack no matter which end is favoured. Starboard tack boats have right of way under rule 36 and those trying to cross on port tack invite retribution from the mass of other right-of-way starters. There will always be the odd exception when some daring helmsman makes a port tack start and goes on to win easily but ignore these strokes of luck. Do not attempt to emulate them.

Try to sail in clear air and with a favourable current aiding you. Your pre-race plan should take into account the wind conditions, the tide changes and the most advantageous side of the course. Once you have decided how the plan should work try to stick with it even though you might be temporarily diverted by other right-of-way boats. But review your plans continually so that quick changes can be made should more favourable circumstances arise.

It is important to sail in clear wind because this is the motive power behind your boat. Sailing under the wind shadow of other boats slows you down and drops you further down the fleet. If you are in such a position, tack away immediately for a short distance until clear air is reached and then tack back onto your original course. This short diversion rarely affects your progess and indeed may bring you out ahead of the other boats who have been content to plod along in each other's shadows. Remember that races are won by those sailing the course in the shortest possible time; this is not always the shortest distance.

Places lost during the first beat are often difficult to regain later in the race so work hard and sail flat out from the moment the starting signal is given. All the boats will close in during the final approaches to the first mark and it is important to ensure that you line up on the right-of-way starboard tack. Boats attempting to get in on port tack are often unable to find a gap and find themselves tacking behind the rest of the fleet. We have already noted that sailing is like chess on water and the helmsman capable of thinking several moves ahead can gain several places.

It is just as important to work hard on what might seem to be the more leisurely downwind leg. Top skippers concentrate on maintaining boat speed and often tack downwind to increase this speed. Split-second timing is needed to gain the favoured inside berth at the leeward marks. If five or six boats are all rounding in line abreast then the outside boat will have to sail a much greater distance; he will also end up to leeward of all the others as they start up the next windward beat. It is a good ploy, therefore, to slow down a little before the leeward mark is reached so that you can sail across behind the other boats and thus gain the favoured inside position.

The finishing line is set between two markers—exactly like the starting line—and on inland courses it may even be in the same place. As each competitor crosses the line he hears a signal—guns, hooters or bells are common—to signify that his race is over. Always make a point of sailing on to the finish no matter how badly things might be going. Other boats ahead may later retire for some reason, some might be disqualified and your finishing position might be much higher than anticipated. In a series of races lasting over a season high finishing positions may improve your final position.

Boat tuning

Many sailors become obsessed with boat tuning in their desire to find extra speed. In many cases this search for the magic ingredient leads them to extravagant lengths, often with no appreciable result. There is certainly some scope for racing dinghies to be 'tweaked up' but superior sailing ability will win far more races than some go-faster gear screwed onto the boat.

Check with your own class rules that your boat has the maximum sail area permitted, that its weight is as near to the legal minimum as possible and that all the underwater surfaces are smooth. Centreboards and rudders should be carefully maintained, particularly when shallow-water sailing might have damaged them.

Make sure that the mast is upright when viewed from the front and raked back about 250 mm or so when viewed from the side. Adjust the rake by first levelling the boat with a spirit level and then hanging a heavy weight from the main halyard to act as a plumb line. The distance this halyard hangs behind the mast at deck level is the measurement of rake. Additional rake can be induced by slackening the forestay and tightening down the shrouds. Make only small alterations to the rake before testing against another boat of known performance.

Jib leads should be adjusted fore and aft until the tension along the foot of the jib and up the leach is about the same. If the boat is fitted with a big foresail which overlaps the mainsail for quite a way then it is usual for the jib fairlead to be moved more aft than usual which 'softens' the leach, and allows the air to travel through the slot more freely. Moving the fairleads inboards makes the boat point higher because it constricts the slot and so speeds up the wind flow. Do not overdo this, otherwise the mainsail will be severely backwinded. Mounting the fairleads on a sliding track enables you to experiment easily with a wide variety of positions.

Hoist the jib as tightly as possible because a firm luff wire is essential for good windward performance. Tightening the jib halyard pulls the mast forward, so allow for this when setting up your mast rake. Adjust the tension of the mainsail both up

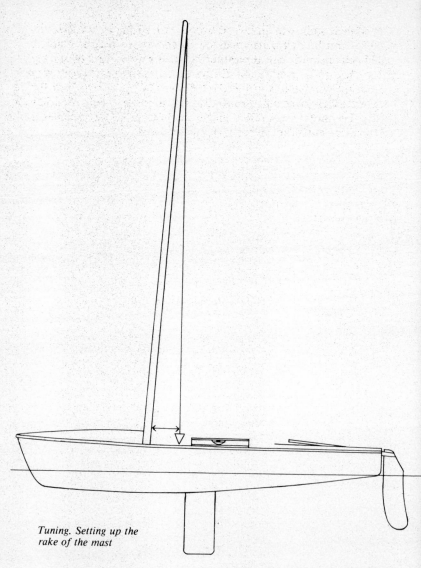

*Tuning. Setting up the
rake of the mast*

the luff and along the foot to match the wind conditions. It
should be set loosely for light airs and progressively tightened as
the wind strength increases. This increased tension flattens the
sail and spills the wind more quickly.

There is a connection between mast rake, sail tension and the
boat's steering characteristics. Too much mast rake or over-

tensioned sails will induce the bows to swing to windwards, which can be tiring and difficult to control in rough weather. This condition is called weather helm. Forward rake or slackly trimmed sails produce lee helm which turns the bows away from the wind and is just as dangerous. The balance to look for is one which gives a neutral feel to the steering in light airs, has just the faintest windward tug in medium airs and becomes a firm pull—no more—when it is blowing hard.

Chapter 15
The Bo'sun's locker

Towing

It is worthwhile buying a boat trailer for it enables you to extend your sailing to other places around the country and abroad. A separate low-loading trolley is needed to get the boat into shallow water. There are many different makes of trailers available, ranging from the de-luxe models with sophisticated independent suspension to cheaper models with transverse leaf springs. All have 406mm × 102mm tyres fitted, though if you own a heavy boat then you should specify heavy-duty four-ply tyres as an extra. There is an advantage in purchasing an extra spare wheel and tyre with your trailer, particularly if you intend making long trips abroad, but do make sure that the tyres match the ones on the trailer.

Trailer chassis frames have either a central backbone with the axle frame forming a 'T' across the rear, or an 'A' frame shaped with the axle forming the base of the 'A'. This latter type is much easier to use because it sits lower on the road and enables boats to be loaded much more easily. The 'A' shape is more readily adaptable to differing hull shapes and, once hitched onto the car, its low profile restricts rearward visibility less. Some mudguards are fabricated from galvanized steel or glassfibre, though most of the better quality trailers use heavy-duty moulded rubber mudguards.

Take great care to ensure that the hull is supported firmly by the central keel chocks, with the side supports just steadying the bilges. These side chocks must not be set too high otherwise the extra loading borne by the bilges can eventually distort the hull. Boat hulls, particularly those made from glassfibre, which have longitudinal cracks along the bilges have almost certainly been subjected to this kind of misuse. The more sophisticated trailers are fitted with full-width padded cradles which match the shape of the hull.

Throughout Europe 50mm-diameter towing balls and sockets are standard equipment for caravans, horseboxes and boat trailers. Some older trailers might still be fitted with two-inch sockets or even the very old inch-and-a-half type. They are incompatible with the 50mm system and should be immediately replaced.

The latest towing regulations permit speeds up to fifty miles an hour to be used if certain conditions are observed. The towing vehicle must display its unladen weight on the nearside (usually on a small card taped inside the window). An oval black disc bearing the figures 50mph must be displayed at the rear of the trailed load. If the combined weight of the trailer, boat and boat contents does not exceed three-quarters of the towing vehicle's weight then speeds of up to fifty miles per hour on de-restricted roads are permitted.

Modern boat trailers handle well at speed and on fast continental roads it is possible to cover hundreds of kilometres each day without strain. Many sailing families load their boats with tents and bedding in order to combine a continental holiday with their boating interests. It is important to pack only soft goods into the cockpit and to take care that the trailer does not become overloaded. It is important, too, that balance should be maintained.

Trailers should only be used for road trailing and not for launching the boat into sea water. However, it is sometimes difficult to transport a launching trolley and the trailer has to serve a dual function. In these instances, make sure that the wheel bearings are pressure greased before and after use so that all impurities are removed. Check the condition of the suspension units, ensuring that they, too, receive regular maintenance.

A relatively new innovation is the Duo trailer/trolley combination. With this system the boat rides permanently upon the launching trolley, which in turn can be easily pulled up a ramp so that it engages upon the trailer. It is quite simple for even a heavy dinghy to be loaded and unloaded single-handed. The best models are finished in a hot-dipped galvanized coating which makes them highly resistant to the corrosive effects of salt water.

Boat insurance

Car insurance policies usually indemnify the owner against all accidents on the road but check that your policy also covers a trailer. In any event, your boat will require insurance cover whilst afloat and this cover can be extended to meet damage caused when towing. Don't be tempted by cut-price policies—the small print restrictions nearly always outweigh any savings made on the basic premium. Insurance rates vary from company to company and, surprisingly, from one part of the country to the next. However, expect to pay around £9.00 for a £400 boat with an additional £1.50 premium for each additional £100 insurace. The policy should cover for at least £100,000 third-party risk and most sailing clubs insist on this as minimum cover. But check with your club before finalizing insurance.

Weather forecasts

Weather forecasts are well worth listening to. Of particular value are the daily shipping forecasts which provide a detailed breakdown of weather conditions around the coast, for they can be easily related to any planned sailing trip. These shipping forecasts use the Beaufort scale to define wind strengths and this scale is understood by yachtsmen around the world.

A study of the Beaufort scale immediately reveals that there is a great deal of nonsense talked when sailors are reminiscing about their battles with the elements. Stories of planing before a force 8 gale become totally unbelievable when you consider that this would involve sailing through waves up to 7.6 metres high. Anything above force 4 or force 5 is too much for a small sailing dinghy and you should make straight for the shore. It is possible to reef down and survive rougher conditions but this would be through dire necessity rather than choice. Force 3 is a suitable wind for beginners.

Spare kit

Keep a small tool-kit aboard your boat so that unexpected emergencies can be dealt with. Some spare shackles, clevis pins, split pins and rigging wire, together with a screwdriver, pliers and a sharp knife should be regarded as the minimum. Keep them all inside a small plastic box which can be taped beneath the foredeck or a thwart. Always keep a spare knife, complete with a shackle opener, in your anorak pocket or fastened with a cord around your waist.

Never assume that every outing in your boat will be trouble-free. The sea inexorably searches out every weakness in the boat and its crew. Learn to be quite self-reliant and equipped to deal with every emergency as it arises. Remember—it may be impossible to get help at the moment it is needed most.

The Beaufort Wind Scale

Beaufort number	Wind speed knots	Wind effect	Sea conditions	Wave height	Max wave height
0	nil	calm	like a mirror	nil	nil
1	1-3	light air	ripples appear	76 mm	76 mm
2	4-6	light breeze	small waves but crests do not break	150 mm	300 mm
2	7-10	gentle breeze	crests begin to break: scattered white horses	600 mm	900 mm
4	11-16	moderate breeze	waves become longer: frequent white horses	1 m	1.5 m
5	17-21	fresh breeze	long waves with many white horses: some spray	1.8 m	2.5 m
6	22-27	strong breeze	large waves with foaming white crests: more spray	2.9 m	4 m
7	28-33	near gale	sea heaps up: white foam is blown in streaks along with wind	4.1 m	5.8 m
8	34-40	gale	moderately high waves with crests breaking into spindrift	5.5 m	7.6 m
9	41-47	strong gale	high waves: crests begin to topple: spray affects visibility	7 m	9.7 m
10	48-55	storm	high waves with over hanging crests: large patches of foam blown before the wind: visibility affected	8.8 m	12.5 m
11	56-63	violent storm	exceptionally high waves: sea completely covered with foam. Small and medium ships lost to view behind waves.	11.3 m	15.8 m
12	64	hurricane	air filled with foam and spray: visibility seriously affected	13.7 m	over 15.8 m

Chapter 16
Storage and maintenance

Carefully maintained dinghies are a pleasure to look at, a joy to sail and always retain a good second-hand value. Planned maintenance ensures that faults are rectified as they occur—which will keep the boat in perpetual seaworthy condition.

Though 'frostbite sailing' is growing in popularity, most dinghy sailors start packing their boats away towards the end of October. Winter storage always presents a problem, for few owners are lucky enough to own a spare garage in which the boat can be left. If the trailer chocks give good overall support to the hull then the boat can be left outside. Place a few wooden battens across the side decks to prevent the cover from sagging, and then make sure that the cover is firmly lashed down around the hull. Tip the trailer backwards, propping it firmly under the towing hitch. Any water which does find its way beneath the cover can then drain quickly out of the cockpit.

The best way of storing outside is to remove the boat from its trailer, take down the mast and turn the hull upside-down on top of some old motor tyres or padded wooden crates. Cover the exposed centreboard slot with adhesive tape and plastic sheeting, otherwise snow and rainwater will seep down into the cockpit and become trapped beneath the decking. There is no need to cover the upturned hull but do make a point of brushing off any fresh falls of snow before it freezes onto the paintwork.

Wooden masts must be carefully supported along their entire length otherwise they develop permanent kinks. Ensure that bare woodwork is first protected with fresh varnish, otherwise winter exposure can damage the mast. Metal masts are much easier to store, but take care that they are not accidentally damaged when left lying beneath the snow. It's worthwhile removing both the centreboard and rudder completely before laying up so that they can be repaired and re-shaped during the winter.

If you own a garage with sufficient headroom, it's a good idea to rig up a multi-purpose block-and-tackle system at each end so that the boat can be hoisted up into the eaves. Boats weighing many hundreds of kilos can be stored this way, but do make sure that the roof anchorage points are firmly secured.

Sails should be gently rinsed in warm water—no detergents, please—and hung up in a warm atmosphere to dry. They can then be smoothed by hand and loosely folded back into their sailbag. *Never* iron sails, even with a luke-warm iron, for this will destroy the set of the synthetic fibres, leaving them limp and lifeless.

Winter is traditionally the time for carrying out major refits and yachting magazines annually feature pages of detailed instructions. But there are few sailors who really enjoy working on an icy boat and there is much to recommend leaving these tasks until the warmer days of spring. Certainly paint and varnish dry much faster and pick up less dust when the weather is warmer.

Varnishing and painting

Varnishing and painting are time-consuming and it is wise to allow at least two weeks for these tasks. All the deck and cockpit fittings should first be removed before washing down the hull and cleaning out the cockpit. All surfaces must then be rubbed down thoroughly and if extensive damage has already occurred, the paint and varnish must be stripped back to bare woodwork. A chemical paint stripper will quickly remove the old coatings but take care to neutralize the stripper with the recommended solvent, otherwise it will continue to work on your fresh paintwork. Paint stripper is best applied with an old brush and left for ten minutes or so. The old paintwork will then start to shrivel away from the surface and it can easily be scraped away with a broad-bladed knife. Old heavy coatings may require two or three applications before the woodwork is completely cleared. Any timberwork which might have become blackened can be bleached back to its original colour using a weak solution of oxalic acid. This can be obtained in crystal form from most chemists and can be easily diluted with water.

After pre-treatment the surface should be sanded down using a medium-grade sandpaper wrapped around a cork or rubber block. This ensures that a flat, even finish is obtained. A high-speed orbital sander gives excellent results though these are quite expensive and rarely found in the handyman's tool-box. Do not use a circular sanding disc attached to the end of a power drill for it will deeply score the woodwork.

Thin the first coat of varnish with the recommended solvent

so that it penetrates the grain. This coat serves as a surface primer and after twenty-four hours can be recoated with normal thickness varnish. Four or five coats will be required to build up a lustrous finish and remember to sand down lightly between each coat. Use wet and dry abrasive paper for flattening down between coats and ensure that the rubbing down paper is kept constantly wet. Leave the work to harden thoroughly for some days before applying the final coat. The surface should first be flattened down using a very fine abrasive paper—400 grit is usual, 600 grit even finer—and then washed over with a clean sponge. The dry surface should finally be wiped with a tack-rag to collect any small bits and then the final coat applied. Apply it thinly so that it flows evenly over the surface. Leave it to dry and resist any temptation to remove suicidal flies—the result will be a mirror-like finish.

The technique for producing a painted finish is very similar except that all the coats will be pigmented. This means that a thicker coating can be built up with fewer applications—usually a primer, two undercoatings and two gloss finishes. Any depressions can be levelled with a paste stopper or filling compound. Rubbing down between coats is just as important for a high gloss finish. Transparent colours such as orange or maroon may require extra coats.

Well maintained boats rarely need such extensive repaints. Minor touch-up jobs, usually carried on as routine throughout the season, are sufficient to keep them shipshape. The temptation to apply coat after coat of paint must be guarded against because eventually this adds substantially to the boat's weight.

Refitting

Check each fitting before screwing it back into place. Replace suspect parts immediately, paying close attention to rudder hangings, shroud anchorage plates, fairleads and buoyancy bag anchorages. Use new screws—preferably stainless steel—and make sure that they bed down firmly in the old holes. Sloppiness may be overcome by using a larger sized screw but never be tempted to plug the hole with a matchstick. If the hole is over-sized then cut around it and glue a complete wood plug into place. Once the glue has hardened, a fresh pilot hole can be drilled and the fitting replaced.

Repairs to glassfibre hulls

Minor damage to glassfibre hulls can easily be repaired with gel coat tinted to match the original colour. This gel coat can be obtained in five basic colours which can be mixed to match almost any shade. Clean away any damaged fibreglass and wash the area with acetone. The gel coat is tinted to match the surrounding colour and only then is the hardener added. This starts a chemical curing process and at temperatures around 20°C the mixture will harden within half an hour, so don't mix more than you need. Trowel the gel coat into the hole with an old knife and then cover the surface with adhesive tape. This ensures a smooth finish which will require only little sanding down. Remove the tape once the gel coat has cured and, with fine wet and dry abrasive paper, polish the surface smooth. Finally burnish the repair with a polishing compound and it should blend perfectly into the surroundings.

Glassfibre boats do scratch, particularly where they have been dragged along the shore. Most of the scratches can be removed with an abrasive polish and the worst marks filled in with gel coat. However, it may be necessary to paint an old hull and the latest polyurethane paint finishes are claimed to be as tough as the original glassfibre. A special glassfibre primer is needed first to ensure that the subsequent paint coatings bond onto the hull. Once this has been applied the procedure described on pages 121-122 for wooden boats can be followed.

Basic knots.

Reef knot.

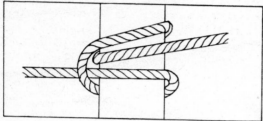

Clove hitch.

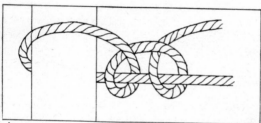

Two half hitches.

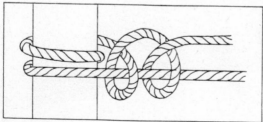

Round turn and two half hitches

Useful Addresses

Royal Yachting Association, Victoria Way, Woking, Surrey GU21 1EQ
National Sailing School, Cowes, Isle of Wight
Sail Training Association, Bosham, Chichester, Sussex
Cruising Association, Ivory House, St Katherine's Dock, London E1 9AT
Ship & Boat Builders' National Federation, 31 Gt. Queen St, London WC2

Acknowledgements

We would like to thank the following people for their help in preparing this book:

Felixstowe Ferry Sailing Club
Waldringfield Sailing Club
Musto and Hyde Accessories Ltd
John Barker
Margaret Fortescue

Index